STATION MASTER

OTHER TURNTABLE PUBLICATIONS:
The World's Oldest Railway
Steam in the North Midlands
A Pre-Grouping Signal Box Album
The Railways of Devil's Dyke
South Yorkshire Railway
East & West Yorkshire Union Railway
Cawood, Wistow & Selby Railway
The Heck Bridge & Wentbridge Railway
Etc.

STATION MASTER

MY LIFETIME'S RAILWAY SERVICE IN YORKSHIRE

by

LEN BEDALE

as told to

C. T. GOODE

1976
TURNTABLE PUBLICATIONS
SHEFFIELD

First Published 1976

© Turntable Publications, 1976

ISBN 0 902844 36 9 (Paper Back)
0 902844 38 5 (Hard Back)

Publisher's Note

It is with deep regret that we have to record the death of Len Bedale while this book was in its final stages of preparation. He will be mourned by all the staff and travelling public who knew him.

Printed by Crown Press (Keighley) Limited, Chapel Lane, Keighley

CONTENTS

MAPS & PLANS

ILLUSTRATIONS

(Between pages 24 and 25)

(Between pages 40 and 41)

(Between pages 56 and 57)

CHAPTER 1

Following in Father's Footsteps

It is said that, to be a true Cockney, one must be born within the sound of Bow Bells; if the same idea held good in my case I could qualify to be a railwayman, for I was born some two hundred yards from the railway level crossing at Norton, near Malton, and in a very short time my parents moved house to within both sight and hearing of three separate and interesting lines of the old North Eastern Railway.

Early in 1914 I can remember being with my father in the Advertising Department workshop, where overtime was being worked, constructing 15 x 20 in. glazed picture frames, which were hung in the waiting rooms of the then numerous stations, and which were greatly in demand by advertisers. The twin-mantled gas light, with its large shade, cast a soft light over the work table; this scene, together with the smell of oak and the stain used, remains for ever in my memory. It was during 1915 that my father volunteered for the forces and was sent to the famous Royal Engineers training camp at Longmoor, before being drafted overseas. In the Spring of 1919 he returned from military service and resumed duty on the North Eastern Railway, where he was employed under the late Mr A. H. Walker, in the Trade Advertising Department, which had headquarters at Malton.

My earliest school years were spent just before and during the period of the First World War, and I finally left during 1922, on attaining my fourteenth birthday. What was not easy to obtain during 1922 and 1923 was work. I had hopes of being apprenticed to a local plumber, but, alas, there were no vacancies. Things looked pretty hopeless, when, early in 1923, a shop and garden helper at a local firm of nurserymen, G. Langster, was found to be required, at the sum of 8/- per week. The firm was well known in the Malton area, the nurseries covering many acres; the shop was large, with good trading connections. Previous to this position I should mention that I had had a 4/- a week post as newspaer boy at W. H. Smith & Son's station bookstall, and the new job at double this amount was a real attraction. The work was interesting and mainly in the open air. Later on in the year, my father was appointed to a supervisory position in the Advertising Department, in London. It was during 1923 that the old North Eastern Railway was merged into the vast London & North Eastern Railway undertaking and trade advertising on the former Great Northern, Great Central and Great Eastern Railways was relinquished by agents and taken over, to be administered directly. This meant, in effect, that there had to be a large-scale reorganisation, in particular at the stations in London, where there was a heavy volume of advertising.

The transfer of my father to his new position created a vacancy at Malton Depot, to which I was lucky enough to be appointed, during November of the same year. The wage was 16/- per week, again doubling my previous earnings. The staff at the Malton Depot consisted of a Chargeman, his assistant, and myself.

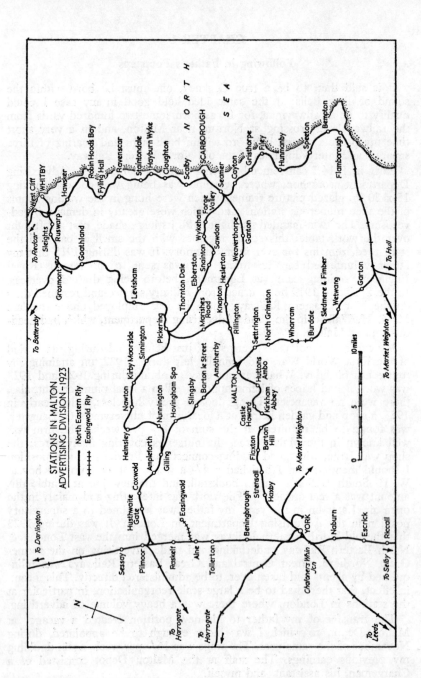

STATIONS IN MALTON
ADVERTISING DIVISION - 1923

North Eastern Rly
Easingwold Rly

My first day of duty was a Saturday, and with the Chargeman, Mr F. Thompson, I travelled to Gilling on the 9.57 am train. I was shown the advertising material displayed on the station platform fences, and later, before returning to Malton, some replacement of the contents of the waiting room frames was done and their glasses cleaned. As Saturday was a half day we retunrned to Malton on the 11.15 am train. On Monday I was sent to Gilling again, alone, with instructions to clean all the enamel plate advertisements, which I did until they gleamed. For Tuesday it was decreed that I should go to Filey, to assist with fixing bill-boards and high-level posters. I can remember well how windy it was. On Wednesday and Thursday we travelled to Scarborough on the same mission. This station carried easily the largest proportion of advertising material in the whole district. The local places of entertainment, such as the Fol-de-Rols. Opera House, Theatre Royal and the Spa, as well as the cinemas, were liberally represented on the poster boards on the station buildings and railings. This meant frequent changes of posters in all weathers. The retaining walls near the running lines were well studded with large enamel plates which required cleaning quite often. Saturday morning was spent locally, renewing the entertainment bills and despatching the same to the stations. Thus ended my first week of employment on the London & North Eastern Railway, and it was fairly obvious to me that my job was going to be quite attractive and unique in its way.

At this point I think I ought to say a few words about my home station of Malton, which was not without interest for railway enthusiasts. First there was the bogie connection between the Down platform and the Up island. The bogie ran on a short stretch of track at right angles to the Down main line. When not in use for letting passengers cross, it was run clear, beneath the platform flagstones of the island side. Control of movements of the bogie was vested in the station signal box. When required for use by passengers crossing to the island platform, or for parcel barrows, the porter, or other member of the station staff, leapt across the track to the bell-push, communicating with the signal box, by which it was understood that the bogie was required for use. If permission could be granted the signalman operated the release lever and the bogie was drawn out on its track by hand and secured with the clamp and hook provided. A wedge-shaped box was then placed in position to overcome the difference in levels and to enable platform barrows to be used. There were some practical difficulties with the whole arrangement, which occurred from time to time. For instance, if a train stopping at Malton on the Down line was of such a length that it fouled the bogie-run and train movements on the Up side were being made, delay could be encountered. Another point was that if the bogie had been inadvertently left in position across the track by the staff after use, it was not always possible for the signalman to get the attention of the ground staff, which made for merciless ringing of the station bell until someone obliged and shot the offending apparatus back to its lair. Occasionally the bogie was liable to leave the track when in motion, and it was quite a strenuous job to re-rail it. Incidentally, the spare bogie formed the principal bench used in our depot!

9

Among other interesting features at Malton was the huge goods warehouse, situated some hundred yards from the passenger station entrance. This building was badly damaged by fire some fifteen years ago. The engine shed was in full use at this period; there were at times some fifteen to twenty engines stabled there. The breakdown unit consisted of a tool van and wooden-jibbed crane, which were stored on a track at the side of the shed. Coal for locomotive use was hoisted in metal trucks from the coaling stage to the engine tenders by a splendid and beautifully-tended steam crane, the pride and joy of its operator. The goods yards were very busy places during those years, with shunting going on until after midnight on most days. During the afternoon, when the local pick-up goods trains were arriving, some with upwards of sixty wagons, one can appreciate the difficulties of clearing the main line, especially during the height of the summer traffic season, with trains following each other in quick succession. The passenger station and yard was also quite a congested area during the holiday season; numerous horse boxes for transfer outside, and mountains of passengers' advance luggage inside — mainly for Whitby. Saturday was always the busiest day, Malton being the changing place for passengers for the Whitby, Driffield and Gilling branches. It was also Market Day. The platforms were packed literally from end to end with country folk. Probably 5.30 pm would be the climax, and when the train due at 5.38 pm (often late) from Leeds arrived and disgorged its Whitby passengers, the congestion was acute. It really had to be seen to be believed.

I ought to state that the total number of stations in the District at that time was 72, and with the addition of Whitby West Cliff and Sessay stations from Darlington District, this was increased even further shortly afterwards. It is indeed a sad reminder that in the current year (1974) only nine of the 74 stations survive in use. Every station without exception carried vitreous enamel plate advertisements. The stations which displayed the fewest signs were Cayton, Speeton, Marishes Road, Hawsker and Levisham, but the inevitable Mazawattee Tea plates, blue with white letters, were at all points and, to a lesser extent, Iron Jelloids, red with white letters. Naturally, the stations showing most advertising matter were visited more frequently. Ganton station, on the York to Scarborough line, had its waiting room chock-full of glazed advertisement frames. It was of course the station for the world-famous golf course of the same name and some of the express trains running between Leeds and Scarborough used to call there. The station buildings on this line, apart from Castle Howard and Malton, had big overhanging roofs. It was customary to have the booking offices and other principal facilities built on the side of the line nearer to the village, to cut down crossing of the tracks on foot. Malton station itself was built of smooth stone, on semi-classical lines and looked quite distinctive. Castle Howard was constructed of cheese-coloured smooth stone with prominent chimney stacks, in a strangely impressive fashion. Castle Howard House was situated some two and a quarter miles away, and no doubt in its day the station dealt with

10

many distinguished visitors, calling on the Howards in their magnificent home.

The stations with "all-over" roofs in the District were Malton, Rillington (the original starting point for the Whitby trains), Pickering, Whitby, Scarborough and Filey. I can remember only one station sporting a canopy which covered the platform, and that was Helmsley. The stations usually had waiting rooms on each platform. Stations furthest apart were Levisham and Goathland at nine miles, the closest being Castle Howard and Kirkham Abbey at three quarters. These last stations were beautifully situated in the Derwent valley, the latter being within sight of the Abbey in question and the sound of the falls.

In the course of my travels I got to know quite a large number of the station staffs. There was, during my early years, a Station-master at almost every station, however small. The first stations I can remember that were placed under the control of one Station-master were Knapton and Heslerton, both on the York to Scarborough line. I can recall travelling with that gentleman, in the sidecar of his motor-cycle combination, when both stations were visited. Sometimes I walked from station to station in the course of my duties, or made use of the local pick-up goods trains, as for example on the Malton and Driffield branch, where passenger services were sparse. It was during late 1924 that the local bus services first made their presence felt, with a dramatic falling away in the number of passengers carried to and from the country stations. Probably the worst affected were those where the stations were situated a long way from the villages served; alas, there were large numbers of these. The fares on the bus services were considerably cheaper than the rail fares and, in some cases, such as between Malton and the "Street" villages, Amotherby to Hovingham, they reached almost cut-throat intensity. It was only on Saturdays that the local trains were really worth running. Some adjustments in rail fares were made, which led to a recovery in traffic, but clearly this falling away was the beginning of the end of the local passenger trains.

In an endeavour to cut down running costs "Sentinel" steam railcars were introduced on the Malton to Gilling branch, but these did not prove very reliable and could not cope with more than one additional vehicle. There were still considerable numbers of horse boxes and cattle trucks conveyed by passenger train. Malton and Driffield trains, for example, had usually some extra vehicles, especially on Saturdays. The news of the reduction in the numbers of passengers had evidently reached the ears of some of our advertising clients, and this led to a large withdrawal of advertising material, both indoors and out. The amount of new fixings was not keeping pace with the removals. At the Malton depot there was a growing stack of the 15 x 20 in. glazed frames, but the loss of the enamel advertisements was offset by the securing of poster boards, chiefly for "Bovril". These were displayed at most stations, but constant re-posting was necessary to maintain a smart show. During 1927 I was called upon to assist in the Leeds District on one occasion. Most of the time was spent in the depot at New Station, preparing the poster boards for despatch to stations. Harrogate was visited two or three times in the company of two men, L. Ward and D. Patrick, employed at Leeds.

I was now approaching the age of twenty, and this was a critical age for male staff at the time; if no other work was available lads, when requiring men's rates of pay, were dismissed and other lads taken on. In addition to this there was quite a large number of redundant adults at various points, following such things as the revision of ticket collecting arrangements, the introduction of steam railcars, which did not require the services of a guard, and the combining of porter and guard duties. The trouble was that there was a general drift of traffic away from the Railway, which was not helpful, to put it mildly.

At York the commercial advertising work was done by the Stores Department man, Mr M. Varley. The depot itself was a huge building, which had formerly been a North Eastern Railway permanent way workshop, situated on the Down side, not far from the ramp of Platform 14. There was a vast store of advertising material here. When I was assisting at York Station I saw quite a bit of the station working and rewarding glimpses of many "crack" trains of the time.

Before I conclude the recollections of the first stages of my career, I should include a few more brief observations, such as comment on that most spectacular route, particularly from the engineering angle, the Scarborough to Whitby branch. Trains in summer were seen at frequent intervals, cleverly timed for, apart from passing loops at certain of the stations, the line was single throughout. There were push-and-pull trains, consisting of an elderly Fletcher tank engine, sandwiched between two equally elderly clerestory-roofed coaches, being driven from inside the leading brake in either direction. This combination obviated the time-consuming process of running round the vehicles in Whitby station and at Falsgrave, outside Scarborough. The outstanding feature of the line was the lofty viaduct at Whitby West Cliff, spanning the Esk Valley and with the line to Middlesbrough and Malton running alongside the river below.

On the main line from Alne to Thirsk the signalling was by Hall's automatic signals. These could be manually controlled in an emergency or for pick-up goods working. The signals were worked by carbon dioxide gas cylinders, in conjunction with track circuiting, and appeared to give reliable service. One uncanny feature about these signals was that, for no apparent reason, on occasion, when no train was approaching, the stop arm would move slowly to the "off" position and just as slowly return to the "on" position.

I obtained much pleasure when working at stations on the Gilling and Pickering branch. Helmsley Station was splendidly built, with a typical North Eastern glazed awning to the platform edge at the main or Down side. There were no less than five waiting rooms incorporated in the station buildings, namely General Room-cum-Booking Office, Ladies' Rooms First and Third Class and Gentlemen's Rooms First and Third

Class. The First Class rooms were quite large and, although more or less out of use by the mid twenties, still bore signs of intensive occupation. One can only conclude that the object in providing these facilities was to segregate the gentry and their servants when at the station. Both Helmsley and Kirby Moorside stations carried a fair amount of advertising matter. The engines used on this line were usually the handsome Tennant 2-4-0s. The same clerestory-roofed coaching stock, based at Pickering and York, was used week in, week out. From the generally substantial appearance of all station buildings it was clear that use of the roads had never been remotely foreseen when the lines were constructed.

On the eve of my twentieth birthday an opening was promised to me at our Leeds depot, because of the unfortunate and prolonged illness of the aforesaid Mr Ward. This meant that I had to move my place of abode to Leeds; but more of that presently.

CHAPTER 2

My first move

Having previously said goodbye to my parents and Malton colleagues, I travelled to Leeds on the early morning train on a certain Monday in August 1928, to take up duties at New Station, my luggage being placed in the depot on arrival. Provisional arrangements had been made with my aunt, Mrs R. Mings, to fix me up with temporary lodging. My uncle was at that time Head Gardener to a Mrs Maude, at a palatial residence known as "The Mount", surrounded by extensive gardens and parkland. The Mings resided at "The Mount" lodge, situated almost opposite Moortown church, separated by the main Leeds to Harrogate road. Compared with all the present-day traffic it seemed very little used! Moortown was a pleasant place in which to live, the area being semi-rural. Each weekday I caught the 7.25 am tram from Moortown Corner to Briggate terminus, some four miles distant, at a return fare of 3½d.

From a work angle the station contained, as one would anticipate, quite a large amount of assorted advertising matter, some of it at the higher levels, making necessary the use of a ladder with two extensions. Many of the large enamel iron plate advertisements, in addition to being high up, were on the station walls over the platform running lines, and these could only have attention when a look-out man was provided by the Engineer's Department. In effect this meant that some scheduled trains had to be diverted when work was in progress. It was quite disturbing when one was perched on top of a high ladder, itself resting on the ballast in the centre of the track, to glance below to find a train approaching the very line (as it seemed) above which you were working, and to find that it was only diverted at the very last pair of points! Almost everything one handled about the station was in a filthy state, especially when fog had descended. Splendid hardwood poster boards, sponsored by the Empire Marketing Board, were sited under the Leeds railway bridges at Lower Briggate, Kirkstall Viaduct in Armley Road and at Kirkgate. The Kirkstall site was some two miles from the depot, very much a case for Drawing and Planning, i.e., Drawing the handcart and Planning the shortest way to get there! The site at Lower Briggate Bridge was actually situated above a recognised stand for an ice cream vendor and, happy thought, after we had moved and replaced the cart to allow billposting, we were usually presented with a free ice cream by the young lady in charge.

Leeds Commercial Advertising District covered the area bounded by Ripon, Pool-in-Wharfedale, Pately Bridge, Cawood and Brafferton to the north and west, with Normanton, Castleford, Selby, Poppleton, Arksey and Copmanthorpe to the south and east. I had the privilege of working at all the stations at one time or another. The larger stations were Harrogate, Ripon, Church Fenton, Wetherby, Cross Gates and Castleford. Cross Gates had awnings on both platforms, and was at that time quite a busy place for passengers. Covered ways extended from the platforms over the footbridges to street level, the place presenting a different appearance from what it does today, gaunt and barren. Tadcaster Station was quite distinctive with its all-over roof and almost ecclesiastical look. Not many passengers there! There was actually some competition with the Leeds City Tramways at Horsforth, Headingley and Cross Gates. At the latter station the tram terminus was quite near, and it was probably here that the competition was most intense. The fares were, I believe, the same (2d), but of course the train was far quicker. On some lines bus competition was stifled by greatly reduced train fares, the 9d third class Day Return fare from Leeds to Castleford being a real bargain. Even in those days first class tickets at 50% more were readily available for those who wished to lash out! All the stations and branch lines were intact.

Almost the only corridor trains were the Leeds-Glasgow and Newcastle-Liverpool through services. A large proportion of the trains were composed of North Eastern stock, some of the brake vans having side duckets, the others with the roof look-out. "Cock lofts" was the staff's name for these. There were vast numbers of coaches which were gas-lit. Some of the really old carriages, even though gas-lit were not fitted with the mantle burners, the light being simply provided by a bare flame about the size of a florin piece. This had to be lit from the roof of the vehicle outside, in fact a large number of the mantle-lit compartments were lit in this way. This could often be a hazardous job for the carriage gas-men and station staff concerned, and more so when the footholds at the carriage ends were covered with ice and snow and the roofs also could be quite treacherous. The gas cylinders were carried below the floor of the coaches and charged with oil gas from storage tanks below ground through reinforced rubber hosepipes. The smell was pungent and lingered long! It was easy to pick out gas-lit coaches, as the pressure gauges were located above the footboards. The gas-making plant was at York, from which place it was conveyed, under pressure, in tanks mounted on wagons painted a bright blue, for easy identification. These wagons were sent by goods train to the various stations where gas charging was carried out.

Trains serving the route from Leeds to Wetherby, Church Fenton and Selby, through trains in some cases, were very poorly patronised, except on special occasions such as Wetherby Race days. Wetherby Station was some distance from the town and it was always to fight a losing battle with the buses. The stations from Thorner to Collingham Bridge were very nicely situated, with a very interesting view of the River Wharfe from the latter place.

I found that the experience I had had in my previous job, both on and off the ground, was a great asset to me. At Leeds New the Majestic Picture Theatre, of City Square, rented a huge poster board, fixed at the top of the two-storey wooden building that housed the ticket collector's and ticket inspector's offices. This board was in a high position and the poster had to be renewed weekly, a Friday afternoon job. If available, the station electrician's wheeled extending tower was used. This looming contraption, though perfectly safe in normal use, made quite an ordeal of climbing up to the poster, plumb vertical, as here a nasty swing developed when negotiating the lightly made top section and it was not an asset to be of a nervous disposition. Extra thrills came when one saw, on glancing below, a four wheeled station barrow, loaded high with parcels, pass about six inches or so from the base of the structure!

After a few days working in Leeds it was nice to be able to get away to the outside stations, those to the north in particular. Probably the stations furthest apart would be Wormald Green and Ripon at 4¾ miles, while the shortest distances occurred between Arthington and Pool-in-Wharfedale, Leeds New and Leeds Marsh Lane and also Holbeck Low Level, both under a mile from the main station. Spectacular engineering works abounded in the area and, commencing with our own place, Leeds New, the whole of the structure was supported by massive brick arches which, when originally constructed, must have been a major undertaking. Actually the River Aire flows under the "Dark Arches", the local term for the underground galleries. The old Queen's Hotel, facing the station exit, was still in existence. Eastwards from the station the lines narrowed to Up and Down tracks only, which were carried on arches to Marsh Lane Station and on through what used to be the Parish church cemetery. Some of the displaced gravestones are still to be seen on the sloping sides of the embankment. However, it was the Leeds-Harrogate route which boasted the most spectacular engineering works in the District. Shortly after passing through Holbeck Low Level Station, there was a steady uphill gradient and, after crossing the Kirkstall road at a high level, the line continued to rise through Headingley and Horsforth stations until some way inside Bramhope tunnel, from where the line began to fall again. The tunnel, which is 2 miles 243 yards long, is a grand example of railway engineering work. Millions of gallons of water were encountered during its construction, which also took the lives of several of its builders. At the north portal of the tunnel there is an impressive castellated facade, unfortunately only visible from the train, no doubt set up to add to the awesome effect. Nowadays the diesel units and diesel-hauled stock make light work of the gradients, but in the twenties the tunnel was usually filled with heavy smoke and sulphurous fumes, and travelling at slow speed a heavy train could take quite a while to get through. There was usually a stampede when one emerged into daylight to get the windows down! At some points water splashed down quite forcefully on to the trains. North of the tunnel and still in the Harrogate direction the Wharfe viaduct sweeping round the valley is encountered, culminating in the truly magnificent Crimple viaduct, some two miles from Harrogate Station.

Harrogate Station was to the Leeds District what Scarborough was to my old Malton area, and much work was carried out there. In the twenties the station was a vastly different building from what it is today. It was brick built, with pretty arches, a light and cheerful place. In the circulating area were quite large numbers of glazed showcases, most attractively and tastefully decked out by local traders, to whom they were let. During the summer months the station was gay with flowers, which were much appreciated. The bath chairs had not entirely disappeared and at the kerbside in front of the station there were a number of "out porters", with their neat handcarts. These men were easily identified by the polished armbands which they wore. If no taxi was available, or if departing or arriving passengers wished to go on foot to or from their hotel, or boarding house, these men could be called upon to convey the luggage. The station railings were adorned with advertising matter, both painted and on poster boards which, both from the point of view of revenue for the LNER and income for the advertisers, must have been a good proposition. Some of the enamelled advertisements must have been displayed for many years; for instance, I can remember one jingle which ran as follows:

"They come as a boon and a blessing to men —
The Pickwick, the Owl and the Waverley Pen."

The interior of the wooden footbridge was literally wallpapered with advertisements which had to be removed and replaced when painting was to be carried out. From the station itself a very frequent service of trains ran to Knaresborough, carrying many passengers to that popular resort. Linking Harrogate with the Capital and with Edinburgh/Glasgow were the Pullman services and some ordinary trains to London, Liverpool and Newcastle.

Late in 1929 the untimely death of our friend and colleague, Len Ward took place. Only in his early thirties, this was indeed unfortunate. His cheerful presence and helpful manner were greatly missed. Although I was quite happy at my work, it was very unlikely that I should get any promotion in my own Department, and without experience in the Traffic Grades I was unlikely to secure even a temporary position in the Service offering promotion. So I realised that I must soon come to a decision. I did mention earlier that I was eager to cast around a little; after further consideration the die was cast, and I decided to move out of the Advertising Department and fill a vacancy for a Signal Lampman at Leeds New, even though the post was rated 4/- a week less basic wage than my current job. Three weeks later I had a brief letter from my Manager informing me that I was appointed and giving the date of my transfer. There was not much comment from my fellow worker, Harry Patrick, who probably appreciated my position.

Rates of pay for a 48-hour week at that time make interesting reading. In 1930 the lowest grades were Porter Grade 2 and Carriage Cleaner with 41/- per week. After this came Station Lampman with 43/-, Signal Lampman and Grade One Porter with 46/-, Relief Porter 48/-, Parcel Porter and Billposter 50/-. Cloakroom Attendant and Ticket Collector Class 2 54/-. Class 3 Shunter Goods or Passenger 55/-. Leading Parcel Porter 56/- and so on up the line until one reached the dizzy heights of being a Foreman Ticket Collector at 65/- or a Yard Foreman (no mean job) at 75/-. The latter position represented to all intents and purposes the highest available position in the Wages Grade. To mere mortals in the lowest Grades, 75/- per week seemed a fabulous amount!

I had a fortnight's training as Signal Lampman, and at the end of this period I took charge. Once more my experience of ladder work proved to be of great value. This time the ladders were made of steel, and were fixtures. The turn of duty was excellent; 7.30 am to 3.30 pm each week-day, including Saturday, and proved to be quite convenient. I was now launched in the Traffic Grades and felt that, at any rate, I had achieved something.

CHAPTER 3

Of Lamps and Leeds

The Signal Lampman at Leeds New had quite a number of other responsibilities each day, in addition to the actual work with the long-burning signal lamps. From 7.30 am to 8.30, except Wednesdays, I was scheduled to help the Parcel Porter on the Top Scale, this being the point on the platform where the market gardeners' and wholesale fruiterers' forwardings were dealt with for rail despatch. Some mornings there were quite large quantities of produce to load on barrows and, later, onto the trains. When there was a lull in the proceedings, opportunity was taken to clean and refill the vessels of the seven buffer stop lamps. The Station Inspectors' and Foremens' lamps, which were rape oil burning and to be found under the desks in their offices, were taken into the lamp room for cleaning and trimming. After 8.30 I was free to get on with the signal lamps. There was an allocation of signal lamps to be attended to each day, starting with the west end of the station yard on Monday, and finishing with the east end gantry on Saturday. The schedule never varied and entailed working on all statutory holidays, when these fell on mid-week days. The lamping duties were usually completed by noon, or a little after. I then had my snack and met the 12.35 pm train from Scarborough, for the purpose of assisting passengers with their luggage. If one was lucky and became free again, the next train to meet was the 12.42 arrival from Newcastle, via Harrogate, which formed the 12.50 to Liverpool. Virtually every passenger assisted gave a tip, and it was indeed unfortunate if I did not secure a job off either of these two trains, especially during the holiday season.

After the departure of these trains I went to the Letter Centre basket, in the Stationmaster's office, to collect Train Notices, signalling programmes and letters for the signal boxes and all staff. This material was usually disposed of by 1.55 pm and I then made a point of meeting the 1.58 arrival from Harrogate. This train consisted of luggage vans and one passenger-carrying vehicle at the rear. With the change of shift of the portering staff at 2.00 pm nobody usually met this train, so if there was any luggage to convey, I was normally the person landed with it! After this, I would usually adjourn to the underground lamp room and clean up the Station Inspectors' handlamps and replace them in their rooms. If it was winter or foggy, I lit the buffer stop lamps, toping them up with paraffin as necessary. Then, all being well, I was free to meet the 3.03 from Scarborough, 3.15 from Hull and 3.23 from Manchester. It only remained to collect my trusty Triumph cycle, clock off at 3.30 and pedal away home. I like the earlier finish.

Following a few weeks in charge, I had a visit from the Clothing Contractor's tailor, who measured me for a new uniform. This uniform arrived about a month later, brand new with LNE/LMS on the coat collar, in embroidered red letters. This splendid suiting was not worn when

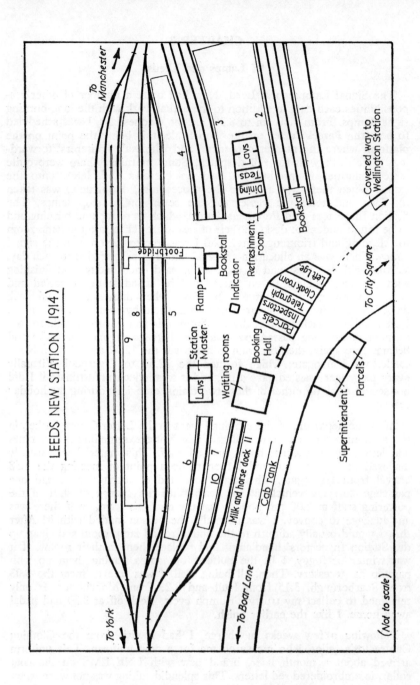

LEEDS NEW STATION (1914)

To Manchester

To York

Covered way to Wellington Station

To City Square

To Boar Lane

1
2
3
4
5
6
7
8
9
10
11

Lavs
Teas
Dining
Bookstall
Refreshment room
Footbridge
Bookstall
Indicator
Ramp

Parcels
Inspectors
Telegraph
Clock room
Left Lge.

Station Master
Lavs
Waiting rooms
Booking Hall

Milk and horse dock
Cab rank

Superintendent
Parcels

(Not to scale)

I was signal-lamping, being donned about lunch time. After being in this job for a few weeks, there was a persistent stench of paraffin about my person and it was impossible to retain much of a shine about my footwear. I decided to wear some old boots while actually on the lamp duties, these being good enough, I thought, for climbing up signal ladders and pounding along the tracks. Actually, they were shabby-looking. This led to quite an unexpected quip from one of the cheery signalmen in the west box, who remarked to me that he only knew one good thing about my boots, and that was the laceholes!

Wednesday was my busiest day; not only was there a larger number of signal lamps to attend to, there were eleven gas and water meters to read and check. Some of these recorded the water supplied to the locomotive cranes and were situated in the very bowels of the station, in the caverns of the Dark Arches. The meter reading record book had to be returned to Mr Maundrel. Another two ancillary duties, not previously mentioned, were the provision of coal for heating the station signal box and the distribution of signal lamp oil to the three lamp trimming huts. The latter operation was arranged with the station permanent way staff Ganger, known as "Paddy" Salmons. The cans of paraffin had to be loaded on to his hand-propelled bogie and distributed to my instructions. The movement of the bogie had to be arranged with the signalman at each of the four boxes concerned, and this could be a time-consuming and tricky operation. Mercifully, the operation only took place every eight weeks or so.

The coaling job for the station signal cabin was another tricky business. I should explain that the cabin in question was tucked away under the eaves of the station roof, over number 7 platform (a through one) and, incidentally, only controlling train movements over the through lines. The first move on the coaling job was to load the special four-wheeled barrow high with coal from the station cellar. The barrow was then brought up on the hoist and moved to the appropriate position on the platform edge, below the signal box, ready for action. The rope provided was threaded through the pulley, and one then had to go back down to the platform in order to find the Station Foreman, to obtain the necessary staff to assist in the task. After the "ground staff" were in position I perched at the bunker, emptied each scuttleful as it was hoisted up, and returned the empty scuttle each time. This was another filthy chore and one had to avoid getting burned by the friction of the rope. However, one got through, and again it would be some weeks before re-coaling would be required. This, of course, depended upon the state of the weather.

Taking things on the whole, though, I liked the job of Signal Lampman. I endeavoured to keep lamp failures to an absolute minimum, this depending very largely on maintaining cleanliness and great care had to be taken to avoid contamination of the signal oil used. In the early days of my duties, I happened to notice one Friday that there were two bad lights on signals inside the station and, on investigation, I found that the wicks below the flame had become encrusted; this meant that there was some impurity in the oil vessels. Casting my mind back to Wednesday, when the lamps had been trimmed in my lamproom, I recalled that, shortly before filling them with paraffin, I had been handling the wicks and vessels of the Station Inspectors' handlamps. At the time, rape oil was used in these and it was evident that either the signal lamp wicks had come into contact with drops of rape oil on the lamp table, or had been polluted by my fingers. New wicks and fresh vessels of paraffin had to be provided; the lamps were lit and replaced in the signals. There was no more trouble from that source!

On the occasions I travelled by train after dark, I was always pleased on approaching or leaving New Station to see my lamps giving a good light. This job of mine was one of the few posts that was not under direct supervision. I knew my duties and performed them as well as I could. The staff who knew the ins and out of my post were few, and when I took my annual leave, the duties were covered by a Parcels Porter named Wilf Hardwick, a previous holder of the position. He was not really enthusiastic when called upon to cover the duties. One of the signals near the east box was situated high above a public thoroughfare known as "The Calls", and when one was perched on the crow's nest on the signal it must have been all of sixty feet to the pavement below. Quite a thrill!

Every fourth Sunday I was rostered for a turn of Grade Two platform duty, 6.00 am to 6.00 pm, with two hours booked off for meals. The duties of the Sunday turn were varied and quite interesting. Usually, 8/- or so was earned in tips for handling luggage, depending on one's luck and also if there were many theatrical companies travelling. This was very much the Theatre Age, and there were still five live theatres open in Leeds. In the early morning, and again at teatime, the platforms had to be swept, seats dusted and toilets given the once-over. All trains were met and from twenty to thirty churns of milk were taken off on a shift. Empties were rounded up during the day, and as many as fifty or sixty churns would be loaded for despatch to the various stations. To me it did not seem a long day, and when finishing duty at 6.00 pm I had the advantage of not having to be back at work again until 7.30 am on Monday, while the others had to start at 6.00 am. Sunday pay was a welcome boost to my earnings.

After being a Signal Lampman for eighteen months, I decided to have a shot at one of the summer vacancies advertised to the staff, in order for them to gain experience. I was now prepared to accept promotion. I had happily steered clear of any injury in my work, though in foggy conditions traversing the sea of tracks could be quite dangerous. Frost on the ladders and on the tops of the signal platforms could also be a serious hazard in winter.

The vacancy I applied for was that of Temporary Passenger Shunter at Malton, at a wage of 55/-, some 9/- above my present rate of pay. Moreover, this was a double-barrelled chance of gaining shunting experience on the one hand, and of residing with my parents for a few weeks. There was a lapse of about two months before I heard a thing, but eventually there it was in black and white from the Stationmaster, to transfer and learn the duties immediately. The keys for the lamp huts were handed over to the reluctant Wilf Hardwick and I travelled to Malton that same day. My parents were extremely glad to see me and it was nice to breathe the cleaner air of the countryside.

One of my friends in Leeds, Bill Riva, the Station Lampman, had given me a few hints regarding the duties of a shunter, in the course of a talk I had had with him some time earlier, and I felt grateful to him at every stage. At Malton I had a few days learning the duties. I found that things had changed since my sojourn there in the twenties. The Malton-Gilling passenger service had ceased, and the Whitby trains were somewhat curtailed. The times of duty in my new job were 5.15 am to 1.15 pm, or 1.15 to 9.15 pm. There were duties other than shunting attached to the post and, believe me or not, one of these was to attend to the signal lamps! When I was on early turn, some of the shunting movements were routine; for instance, the first job was to uncouple the Whitby Road vehicles on arrival of the 5.05 am mail from York to Scarborough. These were left at the Down platform as received and, after departure of the main portion for Scarborough, the Whitby train, which was prepared in the Middle Road siding, went forward, then backed on. The vehicles were coupled up and the whole assembly went forward at 5.55. After this the "Sentinel" pilot engine was available for any local shunting, and most days there were horse boxes to assemble and label for the various stations. These usually went forward by goods train. The signal lamps were dealt with after departure of the 11.24 train to York. So ended the early turn! The afternoon shift was always made up of routine shunts, but usually there were the inevitable horse boxes and special cattle wagons to attach and detach.

I found the information given me by Bill Riva invaluable. For the inexperienced it was not difficult to end up with crushed fingers, when handling stiff couplings and vacuum pipes, or with scalds from the steam under pressure in the heater pipes. Another point during shunting operations is that one should always keep the driver or fireman in view, and if possible warn them if anything out of the ordinary routine is to be undertaken.

During the pre-August Bank Holiday week and the week after, it was quite heavy going. There were several additional return trains to Whitby rostered, the vehicles for which came in penny packets from York and Scarborough, with the result that the sidings were literally choc-a-bloc with coaching stock. When the "Sentinel" shunting engine was available on the early shift, opportunity was taken to assemble the 4-coach trains and place them where they would be readily accessible when required. Incidentally, this tiny locomotive could move up to seventeen coaches (500 tons) on the level — slow but sure in its movements. Just the ticket for people like myself!

I should have mentioned earlier that at the time I was at Malton both my uncles, William Bedale and Jack Middleton were still on the footplate. All the drivers, station staff and, above all, the signalmen in the station signal box were a great help to me and I owe my success in my first venture as shunter to these people. My partner on the alternate shift,

23

Shunter Jack Peacock, had the job at his fingertips and together we were a happy team. In late September I had a brief advice from the Malton Stationmaster, giving the date of transfer back to my permanent post in Leeds, and it was quite a sad occasion when I made my last shunt and went off duty.

1) The Author, as an LNER Stationmaster, at Kirk Smeaton.

24

2) Malton Station, looking towards York. Note the Engine Shed in the left distance.
(T. Rounthwaite)

3) Malton Station, looking towards Scarborough, with the "Bridge" in position.
1.9.56.   (H. C. Casserley)

4) The derelict Castle Howard signal box and site of the former station. 26.8.73.

(M. A. King)

5) The handsome station building at Castle Howard, now a private residence. 26.8.73.

(M. A. King)

6) The foyer and LMS (LNWR) booking office at Leeds New Station, probably taken in January 1935. The locomotive is one of those on the Golden Acre Park Railway, which was closed each winter. (L. Bedale)

7) Tadcaster Station, looking towards Church Fenton. The all-over wood roof is original. 14.6.63. (T. Rounthwaite)

8) The Malton single-coach "Dodger" entering Driffield, with F8 1581 in charge.
(T. Rounthwaite)

9) The Driffield Station shunter, Sentinel 68153, in BR days. A similar locomotive performed these duties at Malton when the Author was a shunter there in the 1930s.
(C. T. Goode)

10) B1 61010 "Wildebeeste" and an unknown A8 4-6-2T on a scenic rail tour at Goathland. (C. T. Goode)

11) **Whitby West Cliff, the most northerly station in the old Malton advertising area.**
   27.4.54. (H. C. Casserley)

12) **Seamer, the first station out of Scarborough on the main line to York. 21.7.73.**
   (M. A. King)

13) Filey. A typical North-Eastern Railway station with all-over roof. 26.8.73.
(M. A. King)

14) Knaresborough station on the Harrogate-York line. Note the interesting signal box beyond the end of the right hand platform canopy. 11.8.73.　　(M. A. King)

CHAPTER 4

Shunting Interlude

I now found myself back in the "Smoke", on my old job and my left hand pocket bulging with the keys of the lamp huts. Wilf Hardwick was also back on his old routine, and all was well. I had changed my lodgings and was now staying with a Mr Ward, in Stoney Rock Lane. It was about this time that I joined the Young Mens Christian Association in Leeds as an associate member, and spent many happy hours within the Albion Place premises. The billiards room was a favourite venue in the evenings, and time passed very quickly. The great billiards and snooker player Leslie Driffield did most of his early play on the tables in the "YM", and I was his opponent on quite a number of occasions. His play, even in those early days, was superb, and to see him engage Mr Berry, the saloon attendant, in play was always a grand spectacle. Sometimes I kept the scores. When I was Leslie's sparring partner, probably 25 minutes out of every half hour were spent fielding! It was obvious even then that Leslie was going to be an outstanding player. Billiards in those days, although perhaps on the wane, was still a popular pastime, and on Saturday nights after the "YM" had closed, we would make our way to Nelson's Hall, in Vicar Lane, which kept open until 11.00 pm. Happy days!

It was not long before I was back in my stride (literally) on the old job. The winter weather was more evident, with much fog and frost, and the Christmas Festival was drawing near. Early in the New Year there was a persistent rumour that the semaphore signals at Leeds New were to be replaced with the then comparatively novel colour light signals; this, if it came to pass, would automatically abolish my job. Here was a matter for very careful consideration and finally I decided to apply for a Parcels Porter's post which was at that time vacant at Leeds. In retrospect my application may not have been such a wise move; it was actually a considerable time before work on the new scheme commenced and the conversion period itself took many weeks. However, the die was cast, and in a short time I was duly advised that I was appointed and absorbed into the Parcels Office staff. The turns of duty were mostly of the late and night variety, early turn being 6.00 am to 2.00 pm, or 7.00 am to 3.00 pm, late was 3.00 pm to 11.00 and nights 9.00 pm to 6.00 am, one hour being taken off for meals. Occasional Sunday turns were called for as well. I was financially a little better off on this job — maybe an average of 7/- a week — and when on late duty not much money was squandered! One of the turns of duty was 6.30 pm to 3.00 am. This turn was detested by most of the men, especially those who lived outside Leeds; in some cases they were unable to get away until the 5.35 train. I myself found the turn quite convenient; I was usually able to push off on my cycle at 3.00 am and was in bed and asleep before 4.00. Rising about 11.00, the rest of the day was mine until 6.00 pm came round again. On this particular turn, general assistance with parcels traffic was rendered until about 8.30 pm; after this I was in charge of the small petrol-driven tractor used for hauling barrows to and from the trains and Parcels Office. This vehicle was not difficult to drive, and after half an hour or so's tuition I felt quite competent to take charge. One of the main things to remember was not to get up too much speed when hauling heavy loads of coupled barrows, in particular when traversing the tortuous barrow way and passage to Wellington Station next door. The platforms too were sometimes quite slimy, which made added caution necessary.

On the whole, things were going quite well with me. My visits to the "YM" were usually confined to weeks when I was on early turn, so sometimes I changed shifts when on late turn, much to the delight of my mates. I did not get in much practice on the billiard-tables, and in consequence my game suffered. During the winter it was decided that classes should be held in ticket collecting duties, and I joined them. In addition I was studying the Rules and Regulations applying to Passenger and Goods guards, with my old friend Bill Riva advising me on the tricky items and likely snags.

The outcome of this was that early in the new year I successfully passed examinations in the duties of both a ticket collector and guard. I felt that the effort had been worthwhile. During the summer months, although not appointed to a ticket collector's post, I was called upon for weeks on end to deputise for one or other of the ticket collectors who were on holiday, ill, or who were themselves deputising for a Station Foreman, or Parcels Foreman. On Bank Holidays, when things were very slack on the parcels side, I, among others, was usually sent to Cross Gates, commencing duty at 5.00 pm, or perhaps a little later, to collect the Leeds tickets from all services, including the return excursions to the seaside. Leeds at this time had no barriers and was thus open from a ticket collecting point of view, all tickets being collected and examined on the trains before arrival. This ruling applied to all trains running from the London Midland & Scottish Railway (LNWR Section), which meant that sometimes it was necessary for collectors to travel to Huddersfield and return to Leeds on the train from which tickets were to be collected.

The period from 1926 to the outbreak of the Second World War was one of mass unemployment. The railways, like many other industries, were feeling the effects of the depression and staffing matters were held to be of first class importance by railway managements. When junior staff had reached the end of their nineteenth year they were often dismissed because there were no adult positions available for them, even at the minimum rate of £2 per week. Their positions would be filled by new entrants to the Service, usually school leavers, starting at the lowest rate of pay. At that time the rates for junior wages staff ranged from 16/- (80p) to 35/- (£1.75), for a week of 48 hours.

I can remember in the early thirties a redundant Locomotive Department Passed Fireman, from Neville Hill Shed, working in Leeds East Signal Box as booking lad, i.e. the boy who entered up the train register book. Similar men were working in a variety of posts away from the sheds and in some cases many months would elapse before a man could be reabsorbed into the Locomotive Department, following the retirement of drivers at the age limit and the general move up the ladder by the remainder.

Generally speaking most of the railwaymen I worked with seemed happy with their lot and accepted the fact that they were better off than vast sections of the community, low as their rates of pay were. In fact, in those days of mass unemployment to be permanently employed on the railway was regarded as being one of the highest aims that a member of the working class could aspire to.

Apart from the basic rates of pay, which in those days compared quite favourably with what was being paid in other industries, at a large station such as Leeds New, most of the staff would be required to perform regular turns of Sunday duty and this provided a much-sought supplement to the normal income. Such occasional casual employment as the Railways offered, although it only paid £2 per week, was eagerly taken up by men from the local Labour Exchange, whose unemployment pay was only about 30/- a week at that time. In those days there were virtually no female employees in the wages grades.

There seemed little doubt in those difficult times that railwaymen were keenly aware that they had comparatively secure jobs, while many of their fellow citizens were either out of work, on short time, or living from day to day not knowing when the axe would fall on their employment. I personally was very conscious of the fact and grateful to be able to say, so far as could be said, that I was permanently employed.

It was now early 1933 and I had completed ten years' service on the LNER. The summer vacancy list had appeared only once and I was tempted (if that could be considered the correct word to use) to apply for a Passenger Shunter's post, Class 2 (60/-), at Leeds Neville Hill, which at that time was the supply centre for coaching stock for North Eastern area workings from Leeds. In due course I was advised that I had been appointed. After a week's training I gave backword and relinquished the post. To put it another way, I felt that I had bitten off more than I could chew. The duties of the post seemed staggeringly hard. Feeling utterly crestfallen I was instructed to report back to my permanent post at Leeds New on the following Monday. Many weeks passed before I felt anything like my old self and I was determined that never again would there be any repetition of this kind of failure. Early in 1935 I applied for a permanent Class 3 Passenger Shunter's position at York, following an earlier application for a summer Passenger Guard's vacancy at Scarborough. I carried out my work steadily and, about a month later, I was advised that I was to be given a trial at York on the Shunter's post. I saw that this would be a real challenge to me as the post of passenger shunter at York had the reputation of being the roughest and most involved in the whole of the North Eastern Region. People like myself, with no knowledge of local and through train workings, were at a particular disadvantage. After a two week's training period I was adjudged capable of being left on my own to cope with the work at the north end, south end and Clifton

Sidings! I found the work to be as hard as anticipated, the layout vast and the moves many, but I had splendid help from my workmates. At the outset, I must have appeared very green to my Class 1 shunter friends at the north end, but I cannot speak too highly of them, and their patience while I found my feet.

All trains which arrived in one of the nine bay platforms at York had to be drawn off by the pilot engine, north or south as the case might be. Some of the trains that terminated at York arrived on a through platform and were propelled by the train engine to Clifton Sidings, almost half a mile north of the station, or dealt with otherwise. Invariably there were complications, such as horse boxes at front or rear, and empty vans or fish wagons to shunt out. Most of the local York-Harrogate, or York-Pickering, trains were stabled at Clifton, or pushed back into the platform ready for early departure, after the release of the train engine. If the train had arrived at the north end, vehicles for south departure were left in the through road for transfer by arrangement, the south end shunters collecting with their pilot, and similarly in reverse. The turns of duty were 6.00 am — 2.00 pm, 2.00 — 10.00 and 10. 00 — 6.00 am. South end had the three shifts while north end had the first two and a day shift of 8.00 am — 4.00 pm. Clifton had exclusive use of the station pilot, which was an advantage inasmuch as any work such as marshalling, or disposal of vehicles, could be dealt with as opportunity offered. The engine crews were quite helpful and, knowing most of the moves, did not accelerate unnecessarily.

The old Locomotive Yard signalbox was the nerve centre at the south end. Quite often moves were made into the station bays, etc. by hand signals, given to the Traffic Regulators from the cockpit on the balcony, to save some heavy pulling of signal levers in the box. At York during those years there were quite a few through carriages to attach and detach. These vehicles contained passengers and were regular booked movements. The train engines in some cases ran direct on to the coaches and were coupled up, then drawn forwards so that the vehicles could be backed on to the appropriate train. It was during one of these movements that I had a narrow shave from being crushed about the head, I was in between the buffers, screwing up the coupling when, for some reason or other, the vehicles were further squeezed together, and when I bent down to get clear, my peaked cap was left in mid air, trapped between the vestibules. Strangely enough, when I pulled my cap away and donned it again, I did not at the time realise the danger I had been in!

A proportion of LNER passenger stock was fitted with the Buckeye automatic coupler. This type of coupler originated, I believe, in the United States. Briefly, the procedure laid down for dealing with them was as follows: if vehicles buckeyed together were to be separated, when the train came to rest the vacuum and heater pipes were disconnected and the vacuum pipe nearer the engine placed on what was termed the dummy plug. The driver had then to create a vacuum and squeeze the vehicles together. At the precise moment that this was done the shunter had to pull the release chain for the coupling, after which the driver was signalled to go ahead. From experience it was possible to determine when the release mechanism had worked. In coupling vehicles, the driver was told what was being done, and after the shunter had prepared the buckeyes on the vehicles, which involved lifting the coupler heads (each weighing about a hundredweight) securing them with the drop-end pins provided, removing the buffer collars and hanging on the hooks, the vehicles were pushed together. If all was well, the automatic couplers engaged. After being tested by a forward movement of the engine, all that remained was to couple the brake and heater pipes and the jumper light cables. In all cases, except when an immediate recoupling was to be done, the coupling heads had to be dropped, the buffers pulled out and the collars on the buffer stems replaced. This enabled ordinary screw couplings to be used, the built-in coupling hook being exposed when the buckeye head was dropped.

Most of the buckeye-fitted vehicles at that time were used on the East Coast main line, though similarly-fitted corridor coaches were also being turned out of York carriage shops for long-distance excursions. These distinctive, green-painted vehicles were greatly in demand, being fitted with bucket seats and permanently fixed tables, very handy for meals and refreshments to be served — Third Open Vehicles (TOV) was their appellation in Company jargon. The Great Western and London Midland & Scottish Railways remained faithful to screw-coupled vehicles to the end of their independent existence.

A Mr Carter was responsible for the shunters. He was stationed in an office close to No. 2 Platform buffer stops. It was to this gentleman that I reported on my first day at York, and after conversation I was presented with a booklet in green card covers — the comprehensive "York Passenger Train Workings"; needless to say, with me it was soon a well-thumbed publication. The Class 1 shunters rarely consulted this booklet; no doubt many had spent their full railway career at York, and knew the workings more or less inside out. Once or twice omissions in the scheduled moves, or transits, were pointed out to me by senior colleagues.

I did mention earlier that I had applied for a Passenger Guard's summer post at Scarborough, and I was in fact appointed as such in late June. This meant a move for no real financial gain or promotion, but in view of the fact that I had applied for the vacancy I decided to let it stand. When I applied I had not known that I would be appointed to the York position. Actually, the job only lasted eleven weeks, but more about that later. I packed my belongings once more, travelled to Scarborough and moved into the recommended "digs".

On arrival at Scarborough I was at once put to "learning the road", which in effect meant travelling over certain lines on which I should be required to take charge of trains. When travelling one had to make notes of special times, all the necessary working moves, and familiarise onself with the signal boxes. My first turn of duty in charge involved signing on at 9.10 am to take the 9.25 Scarborough to Stockton, via Whitby West Cliff, Guisborough and Middlesbrough. This turn had the same coaches,

29

engine and crew for both the outward and return journey. This was a scenic trip indeed, and although one's view of the country and seaside was somewhat restricted from the guard's brake van, I was conscious of the glorious scenery on all sides. I did notice, too, that quite a lot of the commercial advertising at the Stations had disappeared. Could it have been due to an increase in the rates? The weather during that particular summer was generally rather poor, with brilliant sunshine in the early morning, usually giving way to clouds and gloomy skies later, and then rain. It must have been disappointing to the thousands of visitors, as it was indeed to myself.

Scarborough station had its clock tower which dominated the area in the vicinity, and beneath it were the booking and passenger enquiries offices. The layout of the station platforms, except for numbers 3, 4 and 5, was cramped. It was a vast distance from the country end of Platform 1 to numbers 6 and 7, which were originally part of the old goods station. This was transferred to Falsgrave, some half mile away, in order to make room for a new passenger station, which never in fact materialised. Rather a pity, this. Since the thirties, a large part of the roof has been removed in the interest of economy, giving the station a dilapidated appearance to the traveller. However, the station retains one item of interest in having the longest railway platform seat in the world, situated as a fixture on No. 1 Platform, but a platform seat just the same.

CHAPTER 5

Promotion to Station Foreman

Before describing my return to York, I feel I ought to make some mention of the Guard's turns of duty worked from Scarborough. I did describe the 9.10 am shift; the two other duties covered were at 2.20 pm, for the 2.35 relief train to Staintondale and return, followed by the 6.20 Scarborough to Hull, which was worked by a Scarborough guard to Bridlington only, then the 7.10 Bridlington to York, via Driffield and Market Weighton, returning with the 9.20 York to Scarborough, and signing off at 10.25. The third turn involved signing on at 3.15 pm to work the 4.50 Scarborough to Leeds, returning with the 7.25 Leeds to Scarborough, followed by the 10.30 Scarborough to Whitby, as far as Cloughton, where a changeover was made with the guard of the train from Whitby, due Scarborough at 11.02, finally signing off at 11.15. As will be seen, all three turns involved starting the day's work at very gentlemanly hours! I did work one or two Sunday turns, usually to Whitby with evening excursions, which at the time were very popular.

The time passed really quickly. It was late in August when I received an official notice from Mr Dowson, the Station-master, giving the date of my return to the permanent post I had in York. Actually I travelled for two weeks from Scarborough to York and back until I had secured suitable "digs" in York, and was able to give a week's notice at the Scarborough end. The shift at York on my first week there was the 8.00 am to 4.00 pm, at Clifton Sidings. The fact that I was still living at Scarborough meant a long day for me and inconvenience for some of my workmates, because of the adjustments of shift times that were necessary to cover the duties. Sometimes after duty I was quite filthy to travel — one gets one's clothing, hands and face very dirty passenger shunting. At York, probably for this reason, even in those days of low wages and high unemployment, it was sometimes difficult to get staff to take the higher grade duty for an odd day, even though the difference in pay was 2/3d per day compared with the lower grade. As far as I can remember there was only one man who participated and whom I found quite a decent chap.

Work at Clifton Sidings was fairly heavy during my first week on return; I was not familiar with the summer workings! There was an interim period between the summer and winter services when there were large numbers of passenger vehicles to be dealt with, as these came in from the discontinued services. If these coaches were not conveyed to York additionally on the ordinary trains, they were sent by special working to York from other points; the sidings at Clifton were almost full of stock. One must bear in mind that practically all passenger services were composed of locomotive-hauled stock. However, as far as I was concerned, things soon got into their stride and after a few weeks I obtained quite good lodgings off Piccadilly, within walking distance of York station and my work. I found the city quite a pleasant place to live in. Every now and then I would go over to Malton to see my parents. My father was still in the Advertising Department, in a supervisory category, but had now been moved back to York.

After some months there was a vacancy at Malton, this time permanent, in my present grade and I applied for it in order to be able to live at home with my parents. My application was successful and soon I was once more in full charge at Malton. This job was less arduous than the post at York, but it did not offer the scope for higher grade duty. It was now well into the winter service; there were the signal lamping duties to perform each day when on early turn from 5.05 am to 1.05 pm, while on the late turn from 1.05 to 9.05, one acted as guard on the 5.05 Malton to Driffield train, returning on the 7.07, with an arrival in Malton at 7.50 pm. Shunting was the order of the day after arrival; the train I had brought in, usually of only one coach, had to be shunted and coupled to the extra vehicle conveyed on the next day's 6.55 am Malton to Driffield train. This, together with the set to form the 7.44 am Malton to Whitby for the next day was placed in the bay platform and made ready for its travels. After this my engine followed the arrival of the 8.18 pm from Whitby, which conveyed at the rear a through van from Whitby to York. The train set was placed in the Middle Road to form the 5.40 am train from Malton to Whitby the following day, the six-wheeled van being held and attached to the rear of the 8.05 pm from Scarborough to York on arrival. After that, unless there was any other work to do, the engine was dismissed.

Whilst at Malton, I did perform a few duties as guard, apart from the rostered Driffield turn; the 5.00 pm Malton to Hull, for the Fair (Saturday) and often, due to the failure of the "Sentinel" coach, Malton to Pickering, Pickering to Scarborough and return. This latter run was done twice, then one would return to Malton as passenger on the 1.10 pm Scarborough to York. I had "learned the road" from Malton to Whitby with my late sparring partner, Porter Guard George Young, who covered my job while I was absent; also I covered the stretch of line from Glaisdale to Grosmont, on the North Yorkshire and Cleveland branch, but I was never called to work a train beyond Pickering on those lines. The Pickering to Leeds, via Helmsley, and York Annual Shopping Trip, which was actually made up and run from Malton empty, was commanded by the aforesaid George Young, whom I believe looked forward to this trip, which was a complete change for him.

The shunter's duties at Malton were to a great extent routine. Saturday was the most exciting day, for on it was held Malton's weekly Cattle Market. There were usually several wagons of cattle for Nafferton and other such points, plus empty and loaded horse boxes for the wayside stations. These often made the 5.50 pm Malton to Driffield quite an impressive train. I can remember the Station-master at North Grimston, Mr Richardson, remarking on one occasion that he thought the train was the pick-up goods because of the array of extra vehicles conveyed front and rear. When the train had to attach or detach en route there was usually late running on both the outward and return journeys. There was still quite a number of passengers on the Malton to Driffield trains, especially on Saturdays, although during the week schoolchildren were the principal passengers.

I did not apply for any summer period work during the following year, and it was Whitsuntide 1937 before I secured any further promotion. This was to Starbeck, situated between Knaresborough and Harrogate, as Station Foreman, at 58/- per week. Lodgings were obtained for me at 10 High Street, with Mrs Batty, now alas, long since deceased. Her house was only five minutes' walk from Starbeck station, which meant that I was able to enjoy all my meals away from work, booked intervals being given. The turns were: 6.10 am to 2.45 pm, less 35 minutes for meals; 2.45 to 11.15 pm, less a thirty minute meal break; but on Saturdays the late turn was 2.45 pm to 12.15 am (Sunday), less two meal intervals of half an hour each. The Starbeck area, as far as the railway was concerned, was a very different set-up from what it is today, being then a busy and important centre. The Yardmaster, Mr F. Groves, in addition to being in charge of the Up and Down goods shunting yards, the north goods yard, tranship shed and the passenger and parcels station, was responsible for four signal boxes plus one gate box. The passenger station, now an unstaffed halt, boasted three clerks, two station foremen and two porters.

There were frequent trains to Harrogate, Knaresborough and beyond with, in addition, the 7.30 am train from Harrogate to Leeds (7.22 am ex Starbeck) and the 12.20 pm Dining Car express from Harrogate to King's Cross (12.06 pm ex Starbeck). The coaches for these were stabled and cleaned at the Down sidings. There was quite a big motive power depot, providing engines for both passenger and goods requirements. Starbeck was also a sub-depot for the stabling and distribution of horse boxes and coaching stock. Generally speaking, the station was quite busy. On two occasions while I was there, the station was used for the departure and arrival of some of the Harrogate trains, after a derailment at that point had caused a blockage, quite a complicated procedure being involved at such times. From a railway angle Starbeck was always interesting, the original track to Leeds being what was termed the Low line and during this time Starbeck was the only station serving Harrogate, trains from Leeds to the north running through it direct to Ripon. The loop to Harrogate and the York branch were added later. The fares in 1937, in comparison with those of the present day, were extremely cheap, e.g. Day Return from Harrogate to Leeds, 3rd Class, 2/3d; Harrogate to Bradford 3/-; single from Starbeck to Harrogate, or Knaresborough, 2d; and return Harrogate to Knaresborough 7d. There was an interesting ticket-issuing machine on the Knaresborough platform at Starbeck; when it worked correctly it was useful for latecomers and others. It was installed to cover periods when there was no booking clerk on duty at the Knaresborough-side office.

It was the duty of the Station Foreman to cover the booking office duties on the York platform until 8.30 am and after 5.30 pm. It was actually in this office that I sold my first-ever railway ticket to a member of the public. I can remember how crumpled the tickets were after I had

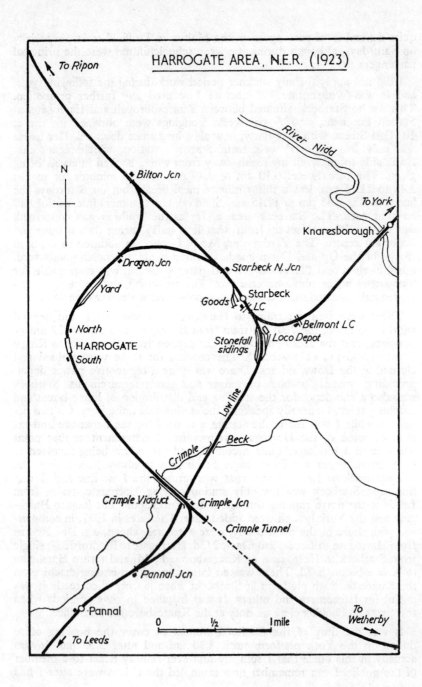

HARROGATE AREA, N.E.R. (1923)

To Ripon

River Nidd

To York

N

Bilton Jcn

Knaresborough

Dragon Jcn

Starbeck N. Jcn

Yard

Starbeck

Goods

LC

North

Belmont LC

HARROGATE

Stonefall
sidings

Loco Depot

South

Low line

Beck

Crimple

Crimple Viaduct

Crimple Jcn

Crimple Tunnel

Pannal Jcn

Pannal

To
Wetherby

0   ½   1 mile

To Leeds

dated them in the ticket press. The knack is in knowing how much pressure to apply when inserting the card tickets in the dating press; in a very short time one can date the tickets with great rapidity, without a trace of a bend in them! To touch briefly on the work of the ticket issuing world, ticket racks in the booking offices of the larger and intermediate class stations, such as Starbeck, contained a fairly extensive range of third class tickets and a smattering of first class, which incidentally livened up the appearance of the rack. During this period also, there were slate grey workmens tickets, and an array of weekly holiday seasons, tickets for the conveyance of dogs, cycles and prams accompanying passengers, ordinary and privilege seasons, miscellaneous tickets such as day, half-day and evening excursions, Pullman reservation tickets, bus exchanges and blanks of all types. Altogether, these made an imposing display! At that time Starbeck used to issue some 55 weekly season tickets to Harrogate, five to Knaresborough and a fair number to Leeds, for the regular passengers.

On early turn the first job on arrival was to get hold of the porter and together sweep the two platforms and the subway, and afterwards dust the seats. These jobs were performed in between other duties, such as attending to trains, issuing and collecting tickets and the like. In addition there were, of course other duties such as reading the gas and electric meters, distribution of signal lamp oil and railway notices to the signal boxes and other staff points. There was no regular porter on my turn of duty, and a constant change of staff had to be contended with. However, any difficulties that cropped up from time to time were somehow overcome.

To bring an end to this part of my saga, I must mention an incident which could have had quite serious consequences, but luckily did not. During the attaching of some empty coaches to the rear of the then 12.25 pm passenger train from Harrogate to York, drawn out of the York siding one day, a large specially made chock of wood was, as was customary, used to wedge the wheels of vehicles left in the siding for attaching. This was in fact the position on this day, but through an oversight it was not removed when the train left with the additional coaches. The result of this was that the bogie wheels of one carriage mounted the chock and seconds later crashed down on to the rails again with a terrific thud. It was several kinds of a miracle that there was no derailment, the Foreman in the North Yard, Mr R. Boston, remarking that we had been very lucky that no derailment had occurred — an understatement. This could be one of the things that happen once in a lifetime.

The Summer Vacancy List appeared as usual, early in 1938; on it was listed Station Foreman at Scarborough at 65/- per week. Apart from the grades of Parcels Foreman at 66/-, and Yard Foreman at 75/-, this was the highest grade and pay rate open to non-salaried traffic employees. I made out my application for the job, and in a surprisingly short time was advised that I was the successful applicant. This was the most welcome appointment that had come to me to date and I was delighted! The date of the transfer, the Saturday before Whitsuntide, was soon upon me. This was the day given to me to obtain lodgings. These had to be arranged by the Station-master, Mr Dowson, and in fact the address could not have been handier for my work, Miss Coultas, 12 Belle View Parade, just two minutes' walk from the station. I was in charge on the following day, Sunday. However, I must recall my Saturday shift (10.15 am to 6.15 pm) with the then Station Foreman, C. Ellis, known to the staff as Charlie. These were actually his last few months on duty, before retirement in October. That day I used quite a few pages in my pocket book, noting the situation of the water, gas and electric meters, names of the staff, capacity of the platforms, in vehicle lengths, and other odds and ends which would prove useful. All very handy for getting the job off the ground, as it were! The two Station Inspectors on the regular staff were George Massender and Fred. Beadle, augmented by temporary summer Inspectors Jack Leckenby, from Marsh Lane Leeds, and Albert Watson, who was normally Ticket Collector at Scarborough. In addition there were two Yard Foremen and Passenger Shunters. I was soon to find out that, due to summer appointments, there was only one regular member of the staff on my shift; he was the station lampman, responsible for the tail lamps and the lighting of the then very largely compartmented rolling stock.

The two weekday shifts of duty for the Foremen were 5.45 am to 1.45 pm; and 1.45 to 9.45 pm. Sunday turns were 4.45 am to 7.45, a short turn of duty, and 10.15 am to finish, usually about 10.50 pm, or even later, less two hours in the afternoon, when there was a lull in the traffic from about 2.30 to 4.30. During the first week of my being in charge there was a gradual build up of traffic, this being the week prior to the Whitsuntide holiday. By Friday there were huge piles of passengers' luggage in advance to be dealt with. All this had to be entered on the vanmens' sheets, before delivery to local hotels and boarding houses. Every barrow was in use; some of the heaviest trunks in Europe must have been in transit at this time! In addition, there were large quantities of fish, both dry and wet, arriving from the harbour. It was a case of all hands to the pump. Saturday was the climax of the week; from early morning most arriving trains were well filled, while in addition there was a huge backlog of advance luggage to get off the premises. Barrows were at a premium and the Foreman was very much in demand.

On occasion, trains would arrive which were too long to be accomodated within the platform length. This could be because of trains having to be supplemented at the starting points, or running out of course, or to local arrangements having to be made in order to clear the running lines for other incoming traffic. The direct results were to cause delay, step ladders having to be used to unload passengers and their luggage onto the ballast, a dangerous and very undesirable process. In some cases trains stopped foul of other lines, which left their plaforms temporarily unusable. Rolling stock was everywhere; the Yard Foreman and Shunters were earning their wages! Sometimes it was quite difficult to keep contact with the staff who, in many cases, had been engaged by passengers to convey their luggage to taxis, or to other trains. Inevitably most excursion and relief trains that arrived had to be moved to the sidings at one point or another. This meant that all carriage windows had to be closed before the trains were shunted. This was quite a job at times, bearing in mind that practically all the coaches used were of the non-corridor type, 10 coaches with 16 windows in each making a normal run of some 160 windows to check. Items left in trains had to be dealt with, and there were quite a few! This day passed very quickly and I was away promptly for once.

At its best Scarborough station was a rambling structure, not easy to work. Trains to and from Whitby used the small new bay platform that had been built at the country end of number 1 and designated 1A. While the arrangement was quite satisfactory from a working angle, as it eliminated the time-consuming procedure of running round trains at the Washbeck Excursion station, it was not an ideal arrangement from a passenger's point of view. In any event platform 1A was quite a long way from either the Booking Office or Ticket barriers. Passengers with luggage arriving at Platforms 7 or 8 were faced with a walk which could not have been much under 500 yards!

CHAPTER 6

Early War Years

At Scarborough station signs that the August Holiday was fast approaching were very obvious, with the large increases in both passengers and their luggage. It was the Whitsuntide Holiday all over again, but on a much bigger scale. Extra help from both the District Engineer's local staff and also Operating Staff from adjacent stations was drafted in for Saturday duty, and they were needed too, for Saturdays were the busiest days, with the departure of holidaymakers in the mornings and new arrivals from late morning onwards. It required considerable planning at times to use these extra staff to the best advantage. In those pre-war days, of course, quite the largest number of visitors to Scarborough travelled by public transport, mostly rail.

At my "digs" in Belle View Parade I was now relegated to one of the attic bedrooms. This was a kind of Rake's Progress, from the Best Bedroom to the Second Best and so on, as visitors and bookings increased. One must bear in mind that I was only paying twenty-four shillings per week for full board; wonderful value indeed! I felt like a permanent resident, meeting quite a number of different and interesting people; there was too a happy atmosphere in the place. During the High Season it was heavy going in the boarding house, with rooms and bookings to allocate. All the work was carried out by Miss Coultas and an aged widow to assist. If one has no idea of what running a boarding house means, then it is an eye-opener when one finds out, particularly when all meals are laid on. I remember one Saturday when I was on late turn, the visitors departing after their stay being bidden goodbye by the lady-in-charge, to be followed at two minutes past eleven o'clock by an avalanche of bedding down the stairs and a hasty preparation for the reception of new guests at noon.

When one considers the staff position at Scarborough in 1938, there were not too many men available. This was made more apparent if anything special cropped up, such as a guard not taking duty, or alternatively, if a search of a train in the carriage sidings, some distance from the station, was needed, for an article left behind by a passenger and reported after the train had been shunted. This in itself meant that a porter had to be instructed and sent; another factor was that as most of the holiday coaching stock was of the non-corridor type, each compartment had to be entered individually from the track, until the item was found, which could be quite a time-consuming operation, the man being a loss to the station until he returned. The lighting of the compartmented stock was another problem too, quite a large proportion of the vehicles on excursion trains, for instance, still being lit by gas, with no by-passes. The station itself was also illuminated by gas, drawn from the town supply, the lights being controlled from a central point by wheel valves. The Left Luggage office and its staffing, especially on Saturdays at the height of the holiday season, was indeed a headache. It was always a relief when, in the late afternoon,

38

the immediate rush was over. I have seen left luggage stored in every corner, and on occasion even within the fireside fender.

While on the subject of left luggage I must relate an incident that happened while I was at Scarborough. Late one Saturday afternoon I was approached by a young lady who was obviously in a state of great anxiety. Her story concerned the loss of her engagement ring, one of those events that happen only once in a lifetime. The young lady in question had travelled from Liverpool to Scarborough, changing trains at Manchester. During the journey from Liverpool to Manchester she made use of the toilet and while washing her hands she remembered removing her ring and placing it on the edge of the washbowl. That was all. When the train reached Manchester she duly changed trains and after the second part of her journey discovered her loss. It was evident that the chances of the ring being recovered were very slim indeed. However, I took full details and put together a suitable telegram to the Lost Property office in Manchester which was duly despatched over railway wires. Surprise! — Surprise! A reply to my message was received later in the evening stating that the ring had been handed in at that point and instructions were awaited. The young lady was naturally overjoyed to think that her ring had been re-covered. The happy incident pleased me too; in fact my heart warmed to think that anyone could have been so honest.

Another story takes me back to the Thursday of Bank Holiday Week, when I was called to the ticket barrier on number 3 Platform by the Ticket Collector on duty, who wished me to give permission for two arriving passengers to pass through the barrier. They had tickets for Blackpool and they had obviously boarded the wrong train at Leeds New. On investigation it was found that the two half-day excursion trains had been tail-to-tail on number 6 through platform, and for some unknown reason they had boarded the LNER train. This was a remarkable example of out-of-course travel — probably the couple concerned had never previously travelled by rail. It is possible that on that particular day the Blackpool ticket collectors had a similar case in reverse!

It was in late August of this year that the international crisis in Europe flared up and the threat of war seemed imminent. This, naturally, had quite a disturbing effect on holiday makers. Local signs were the fitting of canvas-framed screens over the arched windows at the town end of the station, also the whitening of the platform edges. The whole situation was gloomy in the extreme, both locally and world-wide. The situation eased on the drawing up of the short-lived "Munich Agreement", with the then Prime Minister, the Rt. Hon. Neville Chamberlain and the German Chancellor Adolf Hitler. The weather, which was beautiful in September, did much to put a brighter outlook on the closing weeks of the 1938 Holiday Season. My post at Scarborough lasted until early October. Taking things on the whole I enjoyed the break and was quite sorry when the time came for me to make preparations for my return to Starbeck.

October 1938 saw the retirement of my opposite number at Scarborough, Station Foreman Charlie Ellis. Many of the staff were of the opinion that, when his post became vacant, I should be the successful applicant, but I knew that my chances of gaining this job permanently were indeed slim and were proved so when the post was awarded to Mr Coupland, a Passenger Guard at Leeds. Had I been appointed I may say that this book would never have been written, for I should have made my home in Scarborough, which I still think is one of the finest places in Britain. However, this was not to be and early in October I resumed duty at Starbeck, which after the hectic bustle of Scarborough, seemed very quiet.

It was apparent that the railways would never recover the passengers lost to the buses on many country routes, although a large number of the branches were to remain intact for some years. As 1939 progressed the outbreak of war in Europe seemed inevitable; it was only too obvious that Germany was preparing for "Something on a Large Scale". The "Munich Agreement" had indeed been built on shifting sands. In August, and actually before, many preparations had been made on the railways, such as timetables which were drawn up for much-reduced passenger services. There were also far-reaching plans for great increases in goods traffic in the war emergency. Every probability had to be covered, and all branches of the Railway Service were involved.

War was declared on Sunday, 3rd September 1939. I was on duty on that day, at the end of the Summer Service. Like millions of others I had grim forebodings on hearing the very bad news from the Prime Minister over the radio. So far as the railways were concerned, this meant that the emergency arrangements drawn up had to be introduced forthwith. Already from the big towns and cities large numbers of children had been evacuated to the country, mainly by rail. Harrogate was the temporary venue of some Government Departments and large numbers of civil servants were accommodated locally in hotels and private houses. Some of the hotels in Harrogate were requisitioned and life in the Spa town was very different from before. Locally, at Starbeck, the numbers of passengers increased tremendously.

To me, September 11th, 1939 was the most important day of my life, for then I was married to a Thirsk lady, Lucy Ferguson by name. Her family had moved to Starbeck when Thirsk Motive Power Depot closed in the thirties. George Ferguson was very well known as a locomotive driver at Starbeck shed. Lucy and I had originally planned our marriage for later in the year, but in view of the unsettled war conditions we brought the day forward. We had the great luck to obtain a modern house to rent in a nice area, some eight minute's walk from the station and my work. So far as I can remember, this was the last unfurnished house to let I saw in the area for many, many years. I regret to say that we had no honeymoon, for the simple reason that it was quite impossible to get any time off!

From the Monday following the Declaration of War a blackout was in operation, which was absolute, both in theory and in practice. Modifications did follow, but not for several weeks. The passenger station was completely blacked out, a screen being put in position inside the booking

15) Starbeck station, looking towards Leeds. 29.8.72. (M. A. King)

16) Starbeck station, looking towards Ripon. Note the large goods shed on the right mentioned by the Author. 29.8.72. (M. A. King)

17) Kirk Smeaton station, looking east, in 1944. The Stationmaster's house is the two-storey section of the building. (L. Bedale)

18) Sandholme station, looking towards Hull, in the early 1950s. The station was still open to passenger traffic and the original platform awnings are intact.

(C. T. Goode)

19) Womersley station and crossing on the former L&Y line from Knottingley to Askern. The platforms have been removed, but the building is still lived in. It is typical of L&Y stations in this area. 23.11.72.

(T. G. Flinders)

20) Walton station, formerly Sandal & Walton, showing the original Stationmaster's house. The building is now completely demolished. (L. Bedale)

21) Oakenshaw South Junction, looking south. The line diverging to the right foreground is the connection to the former L&Y Wakefield-Goole line. (L. Bedale)

22) Rye Hill and Burstwick station. The two-storey building formed the living accommodation. (L. Bedale)

23) The Withernsea Branch terminus. 31.8.56. (H. C. Casserley)

24) 2-6-0 77000 waiting to leave Hornsea Town, the terminus of the Hornsea branch. Note the typical NER mile post. 31.8.56. (H. C. Casserley)

25) A close-up of the all-over roofed section of Hornsea Town station, after the branch had been converted to DMU operation. (C. T. Goode)

26) Botanic Gardens station, Hull. At the junction beyond the level crossing the line to Hull Paragon diverges to the left and the line to Hessle Junction to the right. The locomotive depot is just off the picture in the left background. 31.8.56.

(H. C. Casserley)

27) A stopping train for Selby, headed by D17/1 1632, leaving Ferriby in LNER days.

(T. Rounthwaite)

28) B16 61478 entering Driffield station on an excursion from Leeds, while another B16 waits to depart.

(C. T. Goode)

office door to prevent light from escaping when the door was opened. It was expected by almost everyone that massive and indiscriminate aerial attack against civilian targets would start at once, but this assumption proved to be wrong and, apart from a single daylight raid by one enemy plane, which dropped a bomb in the vicinity of the Majestic Hotel in Harrogate, causing damage and casualties, the days and nights remained free from air raids. This led to a partial easing of the lighting restrictions on the railway. Hoods were issued to be clamped over the bull's eye of the then rape oil burning handlamps. This was effective but made the lamps clumsy and top heavy in use. The by-passes on the station gas lamps were lit and fitted with a new kind of burner which allowed the flame to play upon about one square inch of mantle. This was certainly a great improvement.

There is little doubt that the lighting restrictions presented great difficulties to the Motive Power Department, both in and out of the engine sheds. The Drivers had literally a hot time; all the vents in the cabs of the tank engines were blocked with tarpaulin sheets and the tender engines had similar treatment. The hazards of driving tender first under these conditions can be imagined. The atmosphere in the cabs with the heat, sulphurous fumes and heated oil must have turned the engines into travelling infernos from the angle of the crews. These were the months of the so-called phoney war, but events were to prove that this was a strategically planned exercise by the enemy. Much bombing of railway property took place during the early forties, but Harrogate luckily escaped attack. Air raid warnings were given to all stations through "control". The preliminary warnings which were given to all stations were termed "purples", and there were plenty of these.

For most of those in civilian employment, fireguard or firewatching duties were compulsory. At Starbeck these duties were not too onerous; on Sundays either from 6.00 am to 6.00 pm or 6.00 pm to 6.00 am on Monday. The command post was the Goods Porters' messroom, and the staff rostered had the responsibility for the goods tranship shed, station and other adjacent buildings. So far as I am aware the locality was never the object of enemy action. The goods tranship shed was huge and largely of wooden construction. A difficult place indeed to guard from fire, for had any incendiary bombs fallen on to the roof, they would have been awkward to tackle, to put it mildly! The passenger awnings were glazed throughout and had any high explosive bombs fallen in the vicinity, they would have been a death trap for anyone standing on the platforms. By 1974 the shed was derelict, though still standing. The passenger station is now an unstaffed halt, an ideal target for vadalism, but more or less intact.

The staff shortages became more and more acute as the war continued, and quite a few Porter Signalmen, Signalmen and others were being appointed to a new grade, which had been introduced with the co-operation of the National Union of Railwaymen. This was Stationmaster Class 6, the lowest previous grade being Class 5. It was created to encourage wages staff to qualify for supervisory positions and at the same time join the

Superannuation Scheme. I was approached by Mr F. Groves, the Yard-master, about the idea and, after considering the implications for some little time, decided to qualify and, in present day terms, "have a go"!

Although I was fairly conversant with passenger station accounting, there were quite a few less obvious subjects to master and, in addition, I had to qualify in goods station work and accounts, of which I had little or no knowledge. I contacted Mr Glover, Chief Clerk in Harrogate goods office, on this score and with his and other help I finally passed the Goods and Passenger Accountancy Examinations. I now began applying for some of the Stationmaster posts and was appointed Acting Stationmaster (Class 6) at Kirk Smeaton, on the old Hull & Barnsley Section, in September 1943.

On the Monday I took charge as Stationmaster at Kirk Smeaton I had quite a long journey, travelling from Starbeck by way of Hull. I had an interview with Mr L. Ballan, the District Operating Superintendent, in his headquarters, which were then situated in George Street, in war-ravaged Hull. Mr Ballan's cheerful manner and encouraging remarks were quite stimulating. After some light refreshment in the now derelict Field's Restaurant, in Saville Street, I caught a train to Doncaster and then to Kirk Smeaton by Messrs Bullock and Sons' bus, alighting at the stop at the bottom of the station approach. By the time I had had a brief look round the station office and signal box it was late afternoon, and I was then conducted to my temporary "digs" by the only other regular member of the staff, Lad Goods Porter Dennis Fletcher. I was back at the station by 8.00 am on Tuesday, my first full day at the new job. Fires were lit in the Station House, in an endeavour to air the premises. Actually Lucy and I had been over from Starbeck on an earlier occasion to see the Station House and its immediate environment. The house was incor-porated in the station building itself and was undoubtedly very solidly constructed, but at the same time very, very shabby inside. Other star features were that there was no piped water supply, no electric light or gas, no bathroom, and the waste from the WC, situated in the back yard, drained some sixty yards to a cesspool in the garden. My wife was naturally daunted by the prospect of moving into such a place, but support me she did and we left our modern house in Starbeck in November 1943. I was now well and truly launched on a thoroughly unfamiliar vocation, ready to ex-perience almost anything.

CHAPTER 7

Stationmaster at Kirk Smeaton

I stayed in lodgings at Kirk Smeaton for three nights before our furniture arrived on the Thursday, a day on which from teatime onwards everything was shrouded in thick, unyielding fog, which lasted for three days and nights. The house had not been occupied for several months and I had to fix up temporary blackout curtains over the windows before we could use a light. We felt utterly done up, and this was not helped by a hanging oil lamp, borrowed from the station office which, after providing illumination for only a few minutes, crashed to the floor when the ceiling hook gave way. I will admit that I ought to have tested its strength first! Apart from the glow of the coal fire and a small oil lamp we had brought with us, we were without light that night; a miserable beginning indeed to my life as a Stationmaster! However, after a reasonable night's sleep, we awoke to the light of dawn, struggling to penetrate the fog-mantled countryside. The blackout curtains were quickly removed and we had breakfast.

The cans of drinking water from Upton & North Elmsall Station had arrived on the pick-up goods train, and Dennis and I placed them in the kitchen. My wife was busy assessing the situation and a cheerful fire burned in the old range, while our daughter Janet, then aged just 2, was playing quite happily. In the meantime I had discovered two old oil lamps, stowed away in the office and, with Dennis's help, cleaned and filled them with some of the precious paraffin obtained earlier in the week from a local dealer. We now had help from an unexpected source with our domestic lighting; Dennis, while attending to the Down Distant signal lamp, happened to mention our plight to a Mrs Rooke, who resided in a caravan near the signal. She loaned us a Tilley mantle lamp, which provided a beautifully bright yellow light, which made the lights of the wick lamps in the living room seem a mere glimmer.

Cooking was done either on the coal range, or on an old oil cooker we had brought with us; the latter, after some repairs by a Kirk Smeaton jack-of-all-trades, named Charlie Elliot, gave us yeoman service. One great snag was the shortage of paraffin oil, which was strictly rationed, but we coped. My wife scrubbed the house throughout, curtains were made and hung, walls cleaned and our new home certainly looked better, though much remained to be done. Local tradesmen were contacted and the travelling shop from Askern called every Friday.

After a day or two we arranged for a regular milk supply from a certain Mr Sanderson (Sandy for short), the dairyman at Norton, some two miles away. Being produced on his own farm, the quality of the milk was excellent, and it was always left regularly, though at first we were at a loss to know when the delivery was actually made. On discussing the subject with the Lad Porter the secret was revealed. My wife and I had noticed quite a number of times that there were subdued flashes of light, in the early hours, in the vicinity of the Station House, but thought little of it, assuming that they were caused by a car reversing at the bottom of the station approach. Dennis told me that after the evening's milking had been completed, the milk delivery commenced, finishing at the Council houses in Kirk Smeaton, at about ten o'clock in the evening. These houses overlooked the station and it was at one of them that an evening rendezvous was arranged, and over a cup of tea, or stronger beverage, the War news was discussed and the Führer's chances of winning analysed. After this it was the custom for the speakers to indulge in forty winks, at the conclusion of which Sandy resumed the milk delivery. It was not everyone who could boast such service at 2.00 am!

Early in 1944 I had a day's leave and we decided to spend it in Leeds. We travelled from Womersley Station, on the former Lancashire and Yorkshire Railway, by the train which left Askern at 7.25 am (7.36 from Womersley) running via Knottingley and returning from Leeds (Wellington) at 5.35 pm. These were the only trains still running over the Knottingley, Askern and Doncaster section. The train terminated at Askern and was stabled there overnight, the engine returning light to Farnley Junction (Leeds) shed. I can remember my wife and I in the early morning, trundling the pram, with our beloved Janet therein, under the dripping trees, along the narrow footpath skirting the road to the station, a distance of almost two miles. It was very pleasant to get into the warm compartment of the train, with the pram duly stowed in the guard's van. On our arrival in Leeds we did a round of the shops, including Lewis's in the Headrow, then a comparatively new store. I can recall the notices exhibited in the windows stating that, in the event of an air raid, the public was invited to make use of the basement as a shelter, as it would be one of the safest places in Leeds, which it probably was. This was, we thought, a kind gesture by the management. Bearing in mind the wartime conditions and the general uncertainty that prevailed, the shops in the city were well set out, the staffs cheery and making the very best of things! We were quite weary on returning home after being away for 12 hours, but we had enjoyed our day and were thankful.

One day after I had been at my new job for about six weeks and had just returned from a gruelling cycle journey to Balne Moor and Doncaster Road Crossings, some 12 miles in all, ridden in a gale, Dennis greeted me at the office door, saying that Parcels had delivered something for me. This was indeed a surprise. What could it be? The parcel in fact contained my complete new Stationmaster's uniform, with neat gold-wired peak cap, exactly the same uniform as was provided for the Stationmasters at the larger stations. I may have been in the lowest grade, but who was to know? After tea I tried on the new clothes and accessories; they were a perfect fit. I was grateful to the Staff Section at the District Office; they had done their work well! One thing I must mention in my account of Kirk Smeaton was our private wood and orchard. My father-in-law came to stay with us, and between us we did a clean-up; the grounds were landscaped and dead trees sawn down. It was a joy to behold! The out-

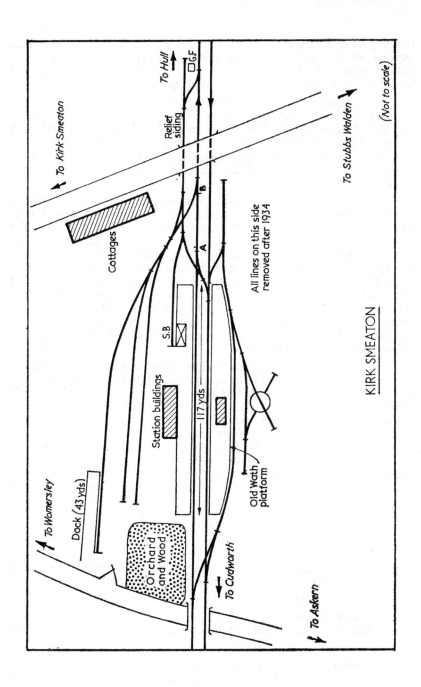

To Hull

G.F

To Kirk Smeaton

Relief siding

Cottages

To Stubbs Walden

B

A

All lines on this side removed after 1934

S.B

Station buildings

117 yds

To Womersley

Dock (43 yds)

Orchard and Wood

Old Wath platform

To Cudworth

To Askern

(Not to scale)

KIRK SMEATON

standing item, if such a term is appropriate, was the large strawberry bed, meeting place of all the birds in the neighbourhood. Nevertheless, we did get some of the berries, and with these my wife made some splendid jam, the like of which I have never since tasted.

We kept contact with the outside world by means of a battery-operated wireless, which again we had brought with us. The war news was indeed grim; the bombing was intensified and on some occasions it was possible to see the huge fires in Hull from our station platform some forty miles away. We were indeed thankful that so far there had been no intensive bombing locally, and this was some compensation for whatever troubles we had.

Workwise I seemed to be making reasonably good progress both in-doors and out. After a little practical help from my colleague Mr T. Shaw (Tom), the Stationmaster at Upton & North Elmsall, the November goods accounts were completed, the balance sheet and numerous forms in support being despatched to the Revenue Accountant, Newcastle, early in December. I must confess that I felt quite pleased that the accounts balanced and that the balance sheet bearing my name was the very first in my new responsibility. Since then in my career I have signed many such documents, and the satisfaction of knowing that all is correct is not without a sense of achievement, when one considers the many returns necessary and thorough check of the books to be made, long before the balance sheet stage is reached.

The only other member of my staff available at Kirk Smeaton station itself was my Lad Goods Porter mentioned previously. There were two Signalmen at Doncaster Road, Messrs H. Carr and E. McQuaid, a female Crossing Keeper, Mrs M. Wilson, at Hazing Lane, situated between Doncaster Road signal box and Balne Moor level crossing, and finally, at Balne Moor level crossing, were two male Crossing Keepers, Messrs Y. W. Horsefield and E. Jubb. The distance by rail from my station to Balne Moor Crossing was $4\frac{1}{4}$ miles, or $6\frac{1}{4}$ miles by road, via sparsely populated countryside and the village of Womersley, with its beautiful church. To Upton & North Elmsall station the distance was $4\frac{1}{2}$ miles, and to Carlton Towers just over nine miles, which incidentally must have ranked among the longest distances between stations at the time when most lines still supported passenger services. In any event, it was the longest distance between stations on the former Hull and Barnsley Railway. From Kirk Smeaton we were able to travel on the local bus services, at very reasonable cost, to Askern, Doncaster and Pontefract, the main local shoping centres. Some of the fares were as follows:-

South Yorkshire Motors:

Doncaster Return 1/4d (6½p)	....	22 miles
Pontefract Return 1/2d (6p)	....	18 miles

Bullock & Sons:

Doncaster Return 1/3d (6p)	....	22 miles
Pontefract Return 1/–d (5p)	....	16 miles

Bargain travel indeed! On Saturdays the buses were usually quite full, there being very few private cars on the road. Groceries were delivered from Pontefract, (Wordsworth's) on Fridays, and the order was called for. There were two shops in the village, in addition to the Post Office. The rent and rates of 11/1d (about 55½p) for the station house were deducted from my salary each week, so that item was well and truly taken care of!

A rough plan which I have included herewith will give an idea of the track layout at Kirk Smeaton, which was a more or less typical rural station set-up. It was possible to do quite a bit of shunting without using the running lines. The exception to this was when vehicles had to be detached from a train arriving from Hull. There was standage for five ordinary wagons only in the Down main between points A and B on the diagram. The vehicles were simply run round by the train engine and pushed into the goods yard as required. During 1944 traffic grew to such an extent that it was found necessary to open the Hull and Barnsley main line for twenty-four hours a day on weekdays, and even occasional Sunday working took place. The years 1944-5 must have been the peak ones for freight.

Most of the coal for shipment via Hull was passing over the Hull and Barnsley, and at Kirk Smeaton these heavily-laden coal trains tore through my station — when they did not tear through one could only assume that all was not well! Occasionally an emergency stop was made to detach defective vehicles, more often than not with a hot axlebox. These stops were usually made during the night, and a loud banging by a trainman at the front door heralded an occurrence of this nature. In effect this meant that I had to get up and switch the signal box into circuit, to enable the wagon to be detached and placed in the station loop for attention. By the time the shunt had been made and the train gone on its way, other trains were more than likely being held at Upton (Wrangbrook) or, to prevent delay, I would accept a train on the Up line from Doncaster Road box. This meant that my cabin had to remain in circuit until the lines in each direction in the section were clear of traffic. Normally, when the vehicles were detached and stationary, the flames from the blazing grease would die down and go out, leaving the axlebox to cool off slowly, without the need for any further action. However, I do remember one occasion when a large petrol tank wagon had been detached for the same reason, with a fiercely burning axlebox. I managed to extinguish the fire in the end with the usual ashes, taken from the track-bed.

I also recall one particular failure of an engine, hauling a long train of coal empties to Cudworth — I think it was the big end which had gone. I opened up the signal box at about nine o'clock and it was three the following morning before I got it closed again! I was there alone with an involved drawing off movement to be made and the disabled engine to be shunted into the loop. There seemed to be more trains than ever that night and, to make matters worse, the relief engine, bringing the fitters from Cudworth, was derailed when leaving the shed, thus creating a further

47

delay, while the heavy tool boxes were transferred to a fresh engine. One can well imagine the lurid language that ensued! Looking at the layout next morning, it was difficult to visualise the activity that had taken place over the track and connections only a few hours previously.

Most of the traffic originating from my station was agricultural — grain, carrots, potatoes and sugar beet, but there was also an important trade in ground limestone, mainly forwarded to Skipton, from the Womersley Graded Stone Company's plant. Arriving traffic consisted to a great extent of seed potatoes, seed grain, fertilisers and fuel. Traffic sent was very much in excess of that received, both in tonnage and value. Some green pea traffic was dispatched during the brief season in mid-July. This was not usually available until about four o'clock on the day of loading; being urgent and perishable, immediate forwarding was essential.

Sheer physical effort was required to handle the grain traffic. The grain was in sacks, weighing two hundredweight (16 stone), or even two and a quarter hundredweight (18 stone). These were manhandled to and from carts and trailers, then loaded or unloaded to rail wagons, usually of the covered type. Most of the farm staff could handle these sacks with ease, but one of the local farmers, Mr W. A. Stephenson of Stubbs Walden, was particularly adept. I have seen 18 stone sacks being loaded by him, carried to the rail wagon like a huge sausage flung sideways over his back. Sheer strength displayed! There was a certain knack in handling these huge sacks; one had to keep one's back and legs rigid when dealing with them. The one hundredweight sacks of potatoes felt like shuttlecocks in comparison. Sheeting wagons with tarpaulins in a high wind was another tough job, more so if one were perched atop a wagon loaded with bales of straw or hay and full to capacity. Dennis and I became highly competent at this sort of thing. Occasionally we had the help of the permanent way staff and Ganger J. Oades displayed marvellous skill in getting the securing ropes as tight as a drum. During one particular day in March 1944 over a hundred tons of traffic were put on rail from Kirk Smeaton, the value of forwarded traffic during that month reaching four figures, which was quite remarkable considering that some of the traffic was consigned at agreed reduced rates.

The passenger service at Kirk Smeaton was withdrawn in 1931, in common with all the other Hull and Barnsley stations west of South Howden. Those between South Howden and Hull survived until August 1955. Examination of copies of the balance sheets at my station revealed that by the late 1920s receipts from passengers had reached a very low ebb. To a certain extent one could understand this, as most of the local population used Askern, Doncaster and Pontefract as their local shopping centres. There never was a rail service from Kirk Smeaton to Pontefract, and it was possible to travel to Doncaster only via Wath, (which involved changing stations at Wath), in the days when the Kirk Smeaton to Wath local service was still in existence. The commencement of local bus services in the early 1920s meant that the end of the tenuous passenger facilities at Kirk Smeaton was imminent. Even in 1943 there were half-hourly weekday bus services to both Doncaster and Pontefract and the buses also ran on Sundays; all buses were generally well patronised. Private cars were almost non-existent, because of the strict petrol rationing. During the time I was at Kirk Smeaton there were no passenger trains and the only time I ever saw passenger vehicles was during a short period when permanent way work was being carried out at Cudworth and a two-coach train ran from Hull to Cudworth each day, transporting the workmen involved.

From the outset of our stay at Kirk Smeaton we were connected with St Peter's Parish Church. Mr S. A. Selby, now the Vicar of Kildwick and Cross Hills, near Keighley, was Lay Reader at Womersley and Kirk Smeaton, which parishes were in plurality at the time, the late Reverend C. E. G. Spencer being the incumbent. Most of Mr Selby's work was done at Kirk Smeaton; it was largely thanks to his efforts that the Kirk Smeaton Youth Club was formed and the youth hut built. Some revival of the work of the Church was apparent. A Sunday School was successfully launched, the first ever at Kirk Smeaton. My wife, together with the Misses Marjorie Woodall and Joyce Molden were persuaded to become teachers in the new venture. My daughter attended from the tender age of two! I served as Treasurer, as well as Stoker-in-Chief for the church boiler for a time. In 1947 Mr Selby was ordained and became curate at Menston-in-Wharfedale. Nicolaus Pevsner mentions St Peter's in his "Buildings of Yorkshire", and has much to say regarding the church of St Martin's at Womersley, a splendid structure, of much character.

The Station House was now much improved internally. The old cooking range in the living room had been removed and a new "Yorkist" range installed in its place. The ancient fireplace in the sitting room had also been taken away and a more attractive tiled replacement put in. The smaller bedroom, overlooking the platforms, was converted into a bathroom, and we were now connected with the mains water supply. It was during the time that the bathroom was being installed that I found out how much an enamelled bath really weighs. Mr Swift, a plumber from Carlton, did most of the work single-handed, but I was called upon to assist in getting the bath up the stairs; this proved a real struggle, but get it up we did! The alterations done were naturally very important to us and only added a few shilling to our rent; even this was very largely offset by the reduced coal consumption, through the modern appliances burning less.

During a very cold spell in the famous winter of 1947 there was considerable hard frost, which penetrated deep into the ground and finally froze our water supply, resulting in our being without for nearly three weeks, which was very inconvenient, reminding us of the early days. The remarkable thing was that when the water came on again the climate was very mild and had been so for several days. The ground had been slowly frozen and was equally slow to thaw out. We were of course without electricity, but this was installed some time after we left. The "Aladdin" lamps we had bought were a vast improvement on the old method of oil lighting, and threw off quite a lot of useful heat. Various minor incidents occurred over the years. A howling gale hit our exposed Station House and the tall kitchen chimney leaned precariously over the house roof for several days, while the gales blew. One morning in 1948 I had two passengers, in the shape of C. T. Goode and K. Bettis, of the Doncaster Grammar School Railway Society who, armed with a brake van permit, wished to join the Down pick-up to enjoy the ride to Howden. Off they went and I knew that they would find the experience an interesting one.

In the meantime at Kirk Smeaton various staff changes had taken place, and there was some difficulty in obtaining a suitable lad for the post originally filled by Dennis. In 1948 I had interviews for posts which were not promotion, and finally, in the name of securing a vacancy with passenger work, I was appointed to the post of Stationmaster at Rye Hill & Burstwick, situated on the Hull to Withernsea line. My wife and I made the difficult journey from Kirk Smeaton to Rye Hill, to look over the station and Station House. This was very old indeed and in all probability was the original residence used when the line was first opened, in 1854. The rooms were small and rather gloomy, the stairs extremely steep and the doors and so forth very crude. The house was vastly different from the Kirk Smeaton premises, which we were to vacate. I remained at Kirk Smeaton until the newly-appointed Stationmaster, a Mr Stanley Fowler, then a clerk at Pontefract (Baghill), and now Assistant Station Manager at Doncaster, arrived. Our removal was arranged by the District Office at Hull, and we were soon installed at Rye Hill & Burstwick, well and truly in the East Riding.

CHAPTER 8

Brief Interlude at Rye Hill

Rye Hill & Burstwick station was situated some three quarters of a mile from Burstwick village, about the same distance from Camerton, on the main Hull to Withernsea road, and about one mile from Rye Hill. Together with Burton Pidsea, some four miles distant, these villages provided our main customers. The countryside round about was almost level, a complete change from Kirk Smeaton, where it was undulating and quite hilly in some areas. We moved into the Station House the day before I took charge. As at Kirk Smeaton the house was part of the station buildings. The rooms faced the station platforms and were rather dark and dismal, particularly the living room. The other two rooms on the ground floor, the sitting rooms, were rather small but a little lighter. The bathroom, which had obviously been added at a later date, was also on the ground floor; it was indeed a dismal place, without any method of heating and must have been the coldest bathroom in Europe! As if in compensation for these poor facilities, there was electric light and power installed, which enabled my wife to bring back into use her electrical appliances, which had so long been out of action. After some months, by a stroke of fortune we obtained a brand new electric cooker.

As far as the indoor work at the station was concerned, I was now experiencing practical passenger accounting for the first time as "the man in charge". This was of course on a relatively small scale, but there was a little of everything; parcels forwarded and received, passengers, season tickets, cartage, and on the goods side the sack returns, plus the goods accounts proper, the compilation of which did not present much difficulty. There was also a small coal sale, for the conduct of which the Stationmaster was responsible. Quite a large number of stations in the North Eastern area had coal sales on the same footing, some large, some small. Briefly, the working of these was as follows: the Stationmaster paid rent through the District Goods Manager for the use of the coal cells, shovels, account books, weighing and other facilities. The coal came by rail, consignments being arranged by the appointed agent, the Stationmaster settling the accounts direct. The porter, or member of the staff responsible, tipped the coal into the required cell, as instructed. The method was that the bottom doors on the wagon were released by the simple mechanism provided, the coal shooting through, after which the heavy doors were replaced by leverage, and the empty wagon sent away, without labels, for further use as required. On taking over a coal sale a representative of the District Goods Manager was at the station to balance the stock books and so on, and when the actual stock of coal had been ascertained, the incoming Stationmaster paid the outgoing man for the coal on hand, at cost, by cheque. Sometimes the amount of cash paid over could run into hundreds of pounds, depending on the size of the sale. In the case of Rye Hill & Burstwick the sale was moderate and there was not much coal on hand. The gross profit on coal at that time was 10/- per ton, bagged and

51

delivered, out of which had to be paid the cell rent and sundry expenses.

There was always the possibility that one of the railway wagons had been pilfered en route, or perhaps some of its load slipped off during a rough shunt; generally, however, the trucks weighed out according to the figures on the wagon ticket or invoice. The weighing scale platforms at some of the stations, including my own, were small, with the result that on occasion farm trailers and the like would not stand wholly on the weighbridge and had to be weighed twice, that is with the front wheels first, then the back ones, when both empty and loaded. This method of finding out the weight was not really accurate and was usually in the buyer's favour. The rent of the coal cells and services provided at Rye Hill & Burstwick when I took over was a nominal (even in those days) £5 per annum. My coal sale was not large, but was worth having for all that. Thorne Colliery's Best and Cobbles were supplied and of good quality; coke and briquettes were also stocked. One advantage of having a coal sale was that one received one's own coal for domestic use at cost!

The Withernsea branch, on which my station was situated, was partly double and partly single line. The single portions were from Hedon to my station, and from Ottringham to Winestead cabin. This latter was situated some half a mile on the Hull side of Patrington. Originally, I believe, the line was entirely double track, the single portions being created during the 1914-18 War, to enable the material thus released to be sent to France, as was the five miles or so of line between Pickering (New Bridge Quarry) and Levisham, on the Malton-Whitby line. Unlike the situation at Kirk Smeaton, almost all the goods traffic dealt with was received traffic. Part of this traffic consisted of horse manure, which was sent from the railway-owned stables at Hull Stepney Goods, to a firm of mushroom growers in the locality. The stench near my home was reminiscent of a racing establishment; however, we did not seem to suffer any ill effects from it, and the mushrooms tasted champion!

Passenger traffic was only moderate; there were a few commuters travelling each weekday to and from Hull and schoolchildren to both Hull and Withernsea. Occasionally there were passengers for long-distance travel. Trains called at Rye Hill between 6.55 am and 10.51 pm on weekdays, and on Sundays, after the end of the Summer timetable, there were two trains in each direction. The Sunday trains in Winter were very poorly patronised and were withdrawn before 1950. I was just getting familiar with the duties of my new post when an entirely unforeseen development took place. I received a letter from the District Operating Superintendent, Hull, stating that it had been decided to couple the station of Rye Hill & Burstwick with Keyingham; the Stationmaster would be raised a Class and would have charge of both stations. This idea of linking two stations was at the time quite an innovation in the North Eastern Region. The combined post was duly advertised, whereupon I applied for it and gained an interview. Some ten days after this I was informed in writing that the post had been awarded to Mr S. Dixon, who had come to Keyingham as Stationmaster a week or two after my arrival at Rye Hill; Mr Dixon had been promoted from the clerical grades. The letter also stated that I should be transferred to the Relief Staff, as Relief Stationmaster, until a suitable alternative post could be found for me. On informing my wife about this, she was most upset and I must say that this was the first time I had seen her cry. To think that our removal and the consequent upheaval had been to no avail. We were instructed to remain in residence in the Station House. Immediately after Mr Dixon had been appointed, he was sent away, on an operating course I believe, for a month. During his absence I was requested to take charge of the dual post, which to me was not a very happy arrangement. There was no clerk at either Rye Hill & Burstwick or Keyingham, and I had to have the assistance of relief clerks for a day or two, to ensure that the month end returns were despatched on time. Later, Mr Dixon had the accountancy for the two stations merged, which meant in effect that one balance sheet only had to be returned for both places.

We had not long been in residence at Burstwick before receiving a call from the Rev. W. Ronald George, Vicar of Burstwick, who had been advised of our impending arrival by the Rev. C. E. G. Spencer of Womersley. We were happy to attend his beautiful church, All Saints. This was what might be termed a homely church, in a picturesque setting. Early in the year its attractive appearance was enhanced by the spring flowers in full bloom in the surrounding churchyard. Here too I took over the Treasurer's post, and the experience gained when I held the corresponding post at Kirk Smeaton stood me in good stead. The peal of bells rung by local lads was, and probably still is, very tuneful. Whilst on church subjects I feel I must say something, however brief, about the churches in the area. The scenery in the large and generally flat plain of South Holderness is not spectacular, but that cannot be said about the churches which lie in this part of the world. Perhaps the most splendid is that of St Patrick, at Patrington, which dates from the fourteenth century and is known as the Queen of Holderness. The graceful spire is considered to be among the finest in England. Hedon, which was a flourishing borough long before the Port of Hull was in existence, boasts the huge church of St Augustine. This thirteenth century edifice dominates the little place. Another church of much interest is the twelfth century church at Swine, and there are quite a few others.

Withernsea and Hornsea are principally seaside towns, and both are worth a visit. The former resort boasts three unusual and widely differing features; firstly the lighthouse which is well inland, only a few minutes' walk from the town centre; secondly the Guy Fawkes Night bonfire which takes place on the sands in the centre of the Promenade and is built up to staggering proportions, pianos and all; the third point is that the town has the odd day of Tuesday for Early Closing. The air at Withernsea is very bracing, in fact there is quite a large convalescent home near the former railway station. The whole Holderness area has now lost both goods and passenger services. The chief feature of Hornsea is Hornsea Mere, the largest inland stretch of water in Yorkshire, and a Mecca for freshwater fishermen.

Most of our local shopping was done in Hull, and we usually travelled by train. On occasion some of our friends from Kirk Smeaton would visit us. The coal sale at Rye Hill & Burstwick was sold to my successor on his return, and I was now officially a member of the Relief Staff. My first assignment was to Skirlaugh and Ellerby stations, on the Hornsea branch, where a Stationmaster's vacancy existed. At the time this was a dual position, where a decision was pending whether to appoint anyone or not. There were coal sales at both stations and the one at Ellerby was quite large. On taking charge, I settled with Mr W. A. Scutcher, who was Relief Stationmaster at Skirlaugh, and required elsewhere, a considerable payment being made. Actually I was at Skirlaugh almost eighteen months and was quite happy with the job. Skirlaugh, with its Victorian style office, was considered to be the parent station.

The station itself was very isolated, the village of Skirlaugh being nearly three miles away. Near the station were two farmsteads, one of them being quite an impressive house occupied by a Colonel Holtby, whom I remember travelled to London now and then, buying his ticket at Skirlaugh. Passengers from the station were few in number as can be imagined, but at Ellerby, where the village of New Ellerby was adjacent to the station, there were more customers. Both stations were staffed by Porter Signalmen. Very few trains stopped at Skirlaugh and in consequence came through the station at speed. The engines drawing the trains on both the Hornsea and Withernsea lines were usually ex-Great Northern 4-4-2 tanks, of LNER Class "C12", with quite noisy coughs on leaving the stations. The coaches were mainly old North Eastern Railway stock, with clerestory roofs and gas lighting. Three-coach sets were the normal working. LNER Class "J" six-coupled goods engines hauled the freight trains, which ran on alternate days on the two branches. Sometimes there were quite hefty loads; on the outward journeys to Hornsea Bridge, vehicles were dropped in the station sidings at Ellerby, and outgoing wagons collected on return.

Shortly before my stay at Skirlaugh ended, a decision had been reached by Headquarters regarding the two stations. Skirlaugh was to be taken over by Sutton-on-Hull, and Ellerby by Whitedale and the coal sales abandoned. When this became known generally among purchasers of the coal, I must admit to having a bit of what is known today as a Bonanza, as all farms stocked up to the limit. When all the coal stocks were sold, the cells and so on went out of use — a shame. I gathered that the Stationmasters taking over did not want the sales. In effect this meant that the tonnage revenue to rail was largely lost, plus the work involving the stations.

My first day away from Skirlaugh was at Flamborough; afterwards I was at Hutton Cranswick, and following this came a week at Hedon. At the time this was an extremely busy station, with two junior male clerks. During the weeks that followed I was at a great number of stations, large and small, in the Hull District. The number of stations to cover which still had Stationmasters was about forty, notwithstanding the recent coupling-up that had taken place. Geographically the District penetrated well into Lincolnshire, the West Riding (including all the old Hull and Barnsley stations) and just over the border of the North Riding of Yorkshire, on the Hull to Scarborough line. Actually there were very few stations I did not relieve at. I remember being at Sledmere and Fimber, on the Malton-Driffield line, during a heavy snowfall which had to be seen to be believed. Bitterly cold it was. The snow drifts were up to the eaves of the weigh office. The local bus services were in difficulties and one evening the Relief Signalman and I had to walk from Garton into Driffield in deep snow, which was being added to every minute! The blizzards over the exposed Wolds country were heavy indeed and the passenger services had been withdrawn some time previously. This was in early 1950.

It was about this time that I was offered the Stationmaster's position at Leadgate, in County Durham, but after visiting it I decided not to accept and to concentrate on applying for posts that I really wished to have. I very much enjoyed being on the Relief Staff; there was plenty of variety and experience of all phases of the work, both indoor and out. Unfortunately, I had no permanent position as such, and was still actually considered to be redundant, which of course I was. I applied to be considered for quite a few Stationmasters' positions, among these being Pontefract (Baghill), Kirkstall, Sandal & Walton, Dewsbury Central, and Newlay & Horsforth. Most of the applications I made produced interviews with the District Managers concerned. Finally I was selected to fill the vacancy for Stationmaster and Goods Agent, as the old LMS termed the job, at Sandal & Walton, which also had charge of Oakenshaw. This put an end to the uncertainty regarding my establishment. Actually, when I was advised in writing of my appointment I was relieving the often vacant post of Stationmaster, Kirk Smeaton, somewhat remarkable under the circumstances!

Sandal & Walton was a Class 4 post, a grade higher than I was, and was really quite a good promotion. A bigger contrast to my previous stations could not be imagined. The Station House, which was detached from the station, had been built in the late 1920s, and was very much like the house at Newlay & Horsforth. Sandal & Walton station, later renamed Walton (Yorks.), was situated on the old Midland main line, some four miles south of Normanton. There were four running lines through the station and as far north as Normanton Goose Hill Junction, where the Lancashire & Yorkshire route from Manchester Victoria, via Wakefield Kirkgate, joined at a trailing junction. When I first went to Sandal & Walton there were almost 200 trains, including light engines, passing through the station every twenty-four hours on weekdays.

The two townships after which the station was named were fairly well separated from each other. Sandal was a residential suburb of Wakefield, also served by Sandal Station, on the Leeds to King's Cross line, while Walton village was adjacent to my station and lay in Wakefield Rural District. We were about three miles from the centre of Wakefield, and travelling there by rail meant a change at Normanton. The village itself was quite picturesque in some parts. The Balk, the approach road leading to the famous Walton Hall, was highly residential. The snag in my appointment was that the Station House was not available. The previous Stationmaster at Sandal & Walton, a Mr L. Kimble, had been awarded a similar position at Tile Hill, near Birmingham. The house there was not vacant and, in consequence, the house into which I was poised to move remained occupied by Mr Kimble and his wife. Eventually this stalemate was resolved.

29) Brough station, looking west. (C. T. Goode)

30) Staddlethorpe Junction. The Doncaster line diverges to the left, while the Selby line goes straight ahead. This is approximately the middle of the longest stretch of dead straight track in Britain. 29.7.73. (M. A. King)

31) **Goole station, looking towards Hull. The River Ouse Bridge is in the far distance. 9.9.73.** (M. A. King)

32) **An early view of Goole Swing Bridge over the River Ouse. Note the signal cabin perched on top of the swinging section.** (British Rail)

33) Bridlington station. A B1 ready to leave one of the excursion platforms on the 6.15 pm to Doncaster. (C. T. Goode)

34) 2-6-0 77010, under the control of a flagman, crosses the station approach at Bridlington, to reach the goods yard. (C. T. Goode)

35) The exterior of Beverley station, one of the largest all-over roofed North-Eastern railway stations. 29.7.73. (M. A. King)

36) An interior view of Beverley station. These handsome buildings were surely the most graceful stations ever built in the provinces in Britain. 29.7.73.

(M. A. King)

37) Drax Hales, a wooden-built architectural gem on the single line from Selby to Goole. Note the country woman patiently sitting under her umbrella waiting for one of the infrequent trains on this line. (P. Cookson)

38) South Milford, between Garforth and Selby on the main line from Leeds to Hull. 29.8.72. (M. A. King)

39) North Howden on the Hull-Selby line. 9.9.73.   (M. A. King)

40) Wressle, the next station to North Howden and near the end of the 18-mile straight stretch from Brough. 9.9.73.   (M. A. King)

41) Reedness Junction on the Isle of Axholme Joint Line, looking towards Goole. The line on the right leads to the terminus at Fockerby, while the train on the left is running down the line towards the junction with the GN and GE Joint Line at Haxey Junction. (C. T. Goode)

42) A diesel shunter brings a train of sugar beet from the Axholme Joint Line onto the Doncaster-Goole main line at Marshland Junction. (C. T. Goode)

43) One of the very few buildings in Britain which was controlled by a railway station-master, but never saw a train — the Ferry Booking Office at Hull Corporation Pier in Nelson Street. Above the clock are carved the initials MSL of the original builders, the Manchester, Sheffield & Lincolnshire Railway, and the date, 1880.

(C. T. Goode)

44) "The Lincoln Castle", one of the last paddle steamers in service in British waters and one of the last coal-fired vessels in the world, approaches Hull Corporation Pier from New Holland.

(C. T. Goode)

CHAPTER 9

Sandal & Walton — My Last Stationmastership

I travelled to Sandal & Walton from Rye Hill & Burstwick on the Monday morning. There was no convenient train forward from Leeds, so I made the journey from Leeds to Sandal by West Riding bus. These buses ran over the original tram route mostly, if not quite all the way. The vehicles were a little unusual in that the passenger entrance was centrally placed. The seats in the lower saloon, to the left of entry, immediately behind the driver's compartment, formed the non-smoking portion. If I remember rightly, the fare for the through journey from the Corn Exchange in Leeds was 11d (4½p). I walked from the bus stop, by Sandal church, through Walton Lane and Oakenshaw Lane, to my destination at the station. Access from Oakenshaw Lane to the station was up a fairly steep, fenced footpath, reminiscent of the entry to the old Beverley Road station in Hull of the Hull and Barnsley Railway. At the top of the slope I was faced with the grim, century-old, stone-built, smoke-blackened block of the station buildings. On entering the station office Mr Kimble, the departing Stationmaster, was waiting to greet me, and after introducing Mr Jack Appleton, the Clerk, we had a walk along the track to West Riding Junction Box. This signal cabin was typical of all five which would be under my jurisdiction. Built completely of wood, with sliding windows, it was a characteristic Midland Railway box, lofty, gas-lit and with the floor lino-covered throughout. This particular box, and Okenshaw South Junction Box, had quite an open outlook, but the three remaining boxes were situated in cuttings. The layout at West Riding Junction was puzzling at first view, but one could soon see its purpose.

After lunch Mr Kimble informed me that he had been told to stay for two days, to give me a chance to make myself familiar with the responsibilities of the post. The day being fine we walked all the way to Normanton, visiting the other boxes en route, including Goose Hill Junction where the old Lancashire and Yorkshire line from Manchester came in. This cabin was actually under the wing of the Stationmaster at Normanton, but could have been involved in single-line working with my yard boxes. Oakenshaw North Junction Box was badly affected by colliery subsidence and the whole structure was leaning away from the tracks to a very marked extent. The local District Engineer had, I understood, been called in, but all that had happened was that a new floor, raised at the back of the box, had been constructed to make conditions more comfortable for the signalmen. In its tilted pose the box proved to be quite a source of interest to passengers who went past for the first time. On Tuesday we toured the colliery area proper, when I was introduced to the Storesmen, with whom I found I was destined to spend a considerable amount of time, much of it in connecting and tracing items missing, or damaged, in transit. On the Wednesday Mr Kimble went off to his new post at Tile Hill, and I was left in sole charge.

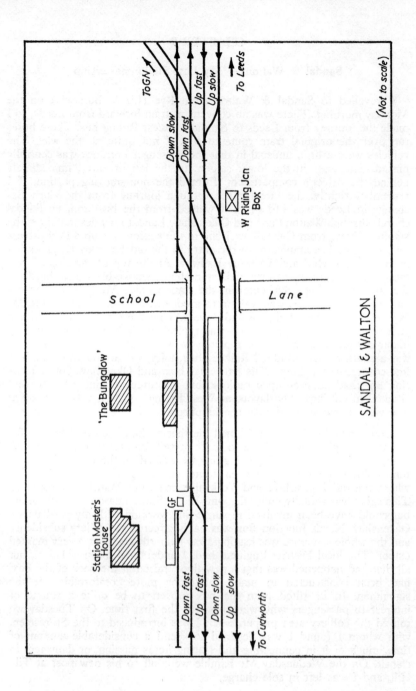

SANDAL & WALTON

(Not to scale)

To GN
Down slow
Down fast
Up fast
Up slow
To Leeds

W Riding Jcn Box

School

Lane

'The Bungalow'

Station Master's House

GF

Down fast
Up fast
Down slow
Up slow

To Cudworth

Jack Appleton, the Clerk, explained the procedure regarding the invoicing of coal, the tracing of missing wagons and general correspondence in connection with those activities. This work was peculiar to stations which had colliery responsibilities, and was something which I had never previously done. Briefly, waybills were written out by hand, with two carbon copies. One copy was retained at the station, the original sent to the receiving point and, finally, one copy was sent to the Accountant, in Doncaster, together with the list of forwarding details supplied by the colliery. The actual carriage charges could then be raised. Correspondence arose with the receiving stations in cases of non-receipt of the invoice or, in some cases, of the wagon! Sometimes the wagons were found to be short weight on receipt.

Apart from the desirability of the Stationmaster being fully conversant with all branches of the work performed at his station, the knowledge acquired in my early days at Sandal & Walton proved invaluable in later years, when clerical shortages were acute and training had to be given to newly-recruited staff, who generally did not stay long at the station, or left railway service altogether.

It was not long before I obtained a real grasp of the Pilot working for the two collieries. The main "Tripper", as it was termed by my staff, left Normanton daily at 2.00 pm, for Snydale and Oakenshaw. At both collieries the loaded coal wagons for the Midland section were placed in position in the access sidings by the colliery locomotives. The wagons intended for weighing were drawn over the colliery weighbridge by the colliery engine. The procession never actually stopped, but moved slowly over the weigh all the time. There were usually three clerks present, one who actually operated the weigh-beam mechanism and shouted out the weight, another to announce the wagon number and tare weight, which was painted on all wagons, and another to jot down the details. The labels were then written out by hand. Sometimes, to save writing, a stamp, prepared from a cut potato, was used to impress upon the tickets words which were often repeated. A junior member of the staff now placed the tickets in the spring clips on the wagons, which were then ready for dispatch.

Three weeks after moving to Sandal & Walton I was called to the Assistant Manager's office at Rotherham Headquarters, for an oral examination on the Rules and Regulations. This touched upon a wide range of relevant subjects, and proved to be a very comprehensive test of my knowledge. At that time the London Midland & Scottish Railway's Signalmen's Block Regulations were still in operation, although the district had been transferred to the North Eastern Region of British Railways. They differed in many respects from the LNER Regulations, which remained in use over most parts of the North Eastern Region proper. For instance, there were more bell signals and different ways of interpreting them. On the LNER, Train Entering Section was two beats on the Block Bell. Under LMS regulations the signal was preceded by the Call Attention signal (one beat). The Block instruments in use were of the rotary type, which in themselves led to more instructions being necessary. My

Assistant District Manager gave me a Pass. He said that it was evident that I had studied the relevant books and I felt pleased that my efforts to absorb the fresh knowledge had been appreciated.

I did mention previously the station buildings at Sandal & Walton, but before passing on I feel that I should say a little more about them, especially as they have now vanished beyond recall. The office windows, indeed all the windows, were set back in their Gothic-type frames; thus the rooms were not very light, even on the sunniest days and, being so high, it was quite impossible to see anything of the outside world through them, without getting to one's feet. When one entered the General Room and Booking Office for the first time, one was surprised by the size of the place; in fact it must have been one of the largest waiting rooms on the line. No doubt it was originally constructed to accommodate rail visitors to Chevet Hall and Walton Hall, also passengers from London and the south changing at Sandal & Walton for Wakefield. Its pointed ceiling and beamed roof gave it an ecclesiastical air. It took painters on their regular visits many days to complete the decorations inside. I may say that all the waiting and other rooms were beautifully kept by the station staff.

Situated as it was in the middle of a busy railway area, "call outs" were quite frequent. They seemed to come along in relays, three or four at a time, then a lull. Derailments usually occurred at points and crossings, whether worked mechanically, or hand controlled, as in marshalling or goods yards. Facing points, when not tightly closed, could be split open by the flanges of vehicles passing over. The extent of the derailment depended to a large extent on the speed of the vehicles passing over, and whether they were loaded or empty. Derailments where locomotives, or tenders, were concerned were obviously more serious, locomotive wheels off the road causing heavy scoring of the sleepers and smashing like egg-shells the specially-made chairs at crossings, making delay in restoration of the track inevitable. One of the most irritating features where derailments were concerned and which sometimes occurred in goods yards and the like, was when the shunter, or guard, involved had made an attempt to re-rail wagons before informining anyone, or calling out the breakdown gang. These attempts, which nine times out of ten ended in failure, only caused further complications, with scored and broken sleepers and shattered chairs.

It was of course essential to find the cause of any derailment reported; sometimes the causes were obvious, sometimes more obscure, or even baffling, but normally the reasons would be apparent from the physical evidence, such as scored sleepers from a particular point, or evidence from the Signalman, if mechanically controlled points were involved. In all my years of railway service I only once saw a derailment actually happen and that was at Leeds New Station in 1932, when an 0-4-4 tank engine had an argument with a set of points in the Through road. There was an unmistakable clank and a rumbling thump, but what the cause was I never heard. Derailments taking place on straight track were quite rare, but I did experience at least two. The first one I was called upon to investigate took place on the Down Goods line, approaching St John's Colliery Box, and was quite mystifying in the early stages. The derailment involved a loaded coal wagon, all of whose wheels had become derailed for no apparent reason. The train of coal wagons had been stopped by signals at the box, and when the signal was cleared the train started normally. Suddenly the wagon sixth from the engine became derailed, nowhere near any points. After a thorough examination of the derailed wagon it was found that a portion of the hand brake gear, which was suspended under the body, had broken away and fallen on to the rails. The wagon's wheels then mounted the metal and were deflected sideways sufficiently to become derailed. The Carriage and Wagon Examiner later found that a bolt, or bolts, had worked loose and fallen out of the apparatus. This derailment, which was a comparatively mild affair, did however cause the Down Main line to be blocked by the breakdown gang, while the wagon was re-railed with ramps. The odds against an accident of this nature happening must be tremendous.

Another derailment took place at Royston & Notton station sidings, during shunting operations. This too was an unusual affair, and no doubt shunting movements of a similar nature had taken place many millions of times previously, in perfect safety. The mishap occurred during the hours of darkness, on a night of strong wind. Three covered vans had been loose-shunted into the Back Road, where they normally came to rest without any further movement. This night, however, the gusty wind had caught the vans, with the result that they ran on, with increasing momentum, and eventually reached the approach to a set of hand points, precisely as two vans destined for the next road had been shunted off. The result was that the vehicles collided in a sideways movement, at a fine angle. Though not completely derailed, in the normal sense of the term, on three of the vans the wheels rose to a height of eight inches from the track at the point of impact, and the vehicles were completely locked together. Surprisingly enough, there was very little damage to the vans, but getting them separated and safely back on the rails presented a tricky problem for the breakdown crew. Derailments have been known to occur for other reasons, apart from collisions and one such, which was quite unique in its way, will be described in the next chapter. After each mishap a "Report of Accident" form had to be prepared, and after completing a few of these, one became familiar with what was required by Headquarters.

By far the most serious accident and derailment which I was called to was one evening at the now demolished Hodroyds & Monckton Main Sidings Signal Box, adjacent to Royston station. A train of thirty, or so, empty coal wagons arrived from the north and came to a stand, by arrangement, on the Up Goods line, with the guard's van clear of the points to the New Monckton Colliery approach sidings. The train was immediately followed by the local pilot engine from the sidings. The train engine having uncoupled, the train of empties was drawn back into the sidings,

61

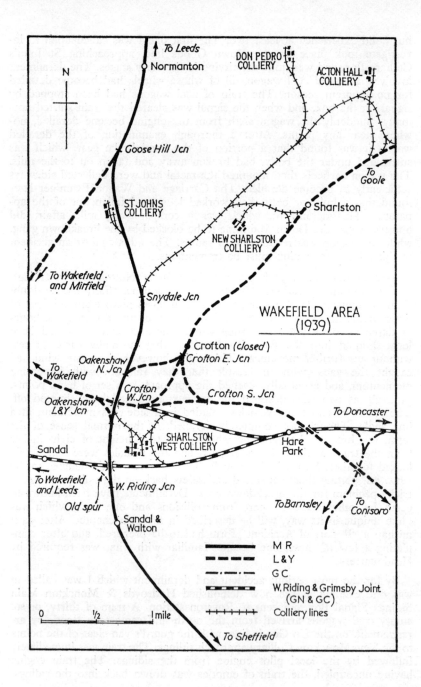

To Leeds
Normanton
N
DON PEDRO COLLIERY
ACTON HALL COLLIERY
Goose Hill Jcn
To Goole
ST JOHNS COLLIERY
Sharlston
NEW SHARLSTON COLLIERY
To Wakefield and Mirfield
Snydale Jcn

WAKEFIELD AREA
(1939)

Crofton (closed)
Crofton E. Jcn
Oakenshaw N. Jcn
To Wakefield
Crofton S. Jcn
Crofton W. Jcn
Oakenshaw L&Y Jcn
To Doncaster
Sandal
SHARLSTON WEST COLLIERY
Hare Park
To Wakefield and Leeds
W. Riding Jcn
Old spur
To Barnsley
To Conisoro'
Sandal & Walton

M R
L & Y
G C
W. Riding & Grimsby Joint (GN & GC)
Colliery lines

0   ½   1 mile

To Sheffield

the guard riding in the brake van next to the pilot engine. I should explain at this juncture that New Monckton Colliery was situated at a higher level than the main line, and if a shunt to the sidings in the Colliery yard was to be made, a good head of steam was necessary to negotiate the sharp gradient. On seeing the ground signal at "clear" the shunt was commenced at a brisk motion. Later it was evident that the points leading to the Goods line had not been closed, and the train was propelled at high speed into the tender of the original train engine, at rest on the Goods line. The resulting impact was tremendous, causing the guard to lose his life in the violent collision.

The Signalman was busy with other duties at the time, and it was a most unfortunate error that he failed to close the points to the Goods line and set them for the Colliery Yard, though the ground signal here was very ambiguous, applying as it did to three directions. There was hardly a wagon of the thirty that had not suffered some damage, such as cracked buffers and severe shock to the chassis. The brake van was badly damaged, and two of the coal wagons were mangled wrecks. The subsequent clearing-up operation lasted all night, with the steam crane assisting. The two wrecked wagons, having had the underframe burnt off by the breakdown gang, were slung on to the adjacent bank, the red and white "Not to Go" labels still attached. The damaged guard's van was placed in a siding until the inquest was completed. The safe working of the steam crane, with its swinging jib fouling the main line, was a tricky business, as trains were quite frequent all night. Like many other derailments, this one did not cause injury to the enginemen, the locomotives themselves absorbing much of the shock.

I remember a terrific gale during the winter of 1955-56, with winds sweeping down from the Pennines with terrifying strength. I was called out to West Riding Junction Box at about 9.30 pm, to try to relight the tail lamp on a Down St Pancras to Leeds express. This was duly done, though not without difficulty. Shortly afterwards, a driver brought his train to a stand at the box, and stated that he had run over some obstruction on the Down Main between Royston Junction and Sandal & Walton. "Obstruction Danger" was sent to Royston Junction for the Down Main, and I sent for the Signal Lineman. In the meantime the wind seemed to have increased in velocity. I entered West Riding box, which was exposed to the full blast of the gale, the whole structure moving visibly and creaking in a disconcerting manner. At times, owing to the movement of the box, it was quite impossible to get the door open; everything was getting a battering! Both Bert Flint, the Signalman, and I feared for the safety of the box, in its exposed position on a high embankment. In the meantime, the Signal Lineman had arrived and together we went on a light engine, to Royston Junction. Walking back together along the permanent way, we met torn down telegraph wires, uprooted bushes and occasional flurries of blinding dust. Soon we discovered the obstruction, like a huge kite down on the track. It was the flat roof of an adjacent permanent way hut, with the wheel marks scored over it by the engine of the driver who reported the obstruction. After a struggle, we succeeded in getting the heavy timber roof lifted off the track and safely dumped. It was now 1.30 am; what wouldn't we have given for a nice cup of tea! After a continuous and exhausting buffeting we reached West Riding box again at about 2.15, informing Bert that the line was now clear. I went back to the Station House, where I found that my garden fence was blown flat, along with most of the plants in the garden, but not our greenhouse, which my father-in-law had soundly bolted down to the brickwork foundations. After making myself a little refreshment, I went upstairs to where my wife and daughter, after a sleepless night, were awaiting my return and expecting the roof to disappear at every moment! There were evidently more guts in the structure than was at first thought and we had no need to worry. Next day we heard that the damage had been widespread, with hoardings demolished and telegraph poles and wires down.

My station had always been well known for its cleanliness and beautiful floral displays, and really one could say that the latter was one of its outstanding features. In the Coronation Year of 1953 we were successful in gaining the Coronation Prize and Shield, awarded to the best station in the Rotherham District. In the face of intense competition from stations in other parts of the District, including the Hope Valley Line, the judges thought fit to award first prize to our station. It was gratifying to know that the efforts of my staff had been rewarded in no uncertain manner. Female Porter Mrs M. Iveson thought up the idea of having two old bread baking bowls, some two feet in diameter, on each landing of the station footbridge. She persuaded the Signal Lineman to bore two holes in each for drainage; they were then filled with potting soil and planted with red, white and blue petunias. These grew nicely and looked neat. I believe another factor which really caught the imagination of the judges were the window boxes, filled with dwarf sweet pea plants, again in the national colours, supported with almost invisible twigs; these, too, looked most attractive. I must say that the idea of the sweet peas in the window boxes was suggested by my wife. At that time dwarf sweet peas were almost an innovation, and proved to be a winner indeed. The only worry was the hanging baskets, the plants in which had to be replaced after being blown away by a strong wind one night.

By way of a change I must tell of another incident which, though not serious in a sense, could have caused delay to the Royal train, which was travelling south from Scotland overnight. About two hours before the train was due, I had a message from the Signalman at Oakenshaw South Junction that the green spectacle glass had fallen out of the Up Home signal and shattered. I immediately sent the Porter for the Signal Lineman, and shortly afterwards he came back to tell me that the Lineman was not available. Action was required. I procured a green flag from the stores cupboard, made my way to Oakenshaw South, climbed the signal and carefully tied the green flag round and over the vacant space in the spectacle and hoped for the best. It worked! There was no delay to the Train of Trains!

Late in 1956 it was evident that staff shortages were getting worse. My staff had declined considerably, and there was now only one Female Porter at the station, working alternately with the Clerk. It was extremely difficult to fill the Clerk's position and, as no Relief Clerk was available, it was necessary for Mrs Iveson and I to cover the job between us, week after week. Coal invoicing had trebled in quantity since the work in connection with New Monckton Coke Ovens had been completed and the Colliery output had been transferred to my station from Royston & Notton. Outside, the shunting staff had been reduced to three and the work at Oakenshaw had actually increased, with the sidings being full of wagons at various times. Opencast coal from a nearby site was also being sent by rail, being tipped into wagons at Oakenshaw, in the high dock.

Passenger traffic had, however, declined (not in numbers, but in terms of revenue). New period tickets, and other cheaper holiday fares, had been introduced from adjacent stations, but my own station was not included, with the result that local tickets only were being purchased, passengers preferring to buy their tickets for longer journeys at the lower prices offered at other local stations. In addition, local commuting to Rotherham had ceased almost completely. However, we continued to obtain what revenue we could. The local parcel delivery had also ceased, traffic formerly delivered by my porter now being delivered from Wakefield by British Railways parcels delivery service. To render matters more confusing, some dunderhead had renamed the station "Walton", the Sandal being dropped. This was very foolish, in view of the large number of Waltons, so, to amend matters, "Yorks." was added, but I never saw why any alteration had to be made at all. Sandal Station was eventually closed, the remaining commercial interests of both Sandal and Hare Park Stations being placed under my control.

Before concluding this chapter, I must record an incident which was not without its funny side. It was noticed by the West Riding Junction Box signalman that one of the doors of a covered container, mounted on a flat wagon, on an early morning goods train, had come open. The train was stopped by signals at Oakenshaw South Junction, to enable the offending door to be closed by the guard. The rather quick stop which had been made had jolted some of the contents of the container on to the track. On taking duty, I was called upon to see what could be salvaged, and on approaching the place where the goods had scattered, I saw a fantastic sight. Dozens of birds, mainly crows and starlings, were swooping down on the track, and rising again in waves. They were obviously eating what had fallen, which proved to be hundreds of brilliantly coloured pills and capsules. There were red, white, brown and yellow pills, and many other varieties. I picked up the containers and took the unbroken ones to the Station Office. In the meantime, when I was moving away, the birds returned, gorging themselves with the items left. One could only hope that they were not lethal!

It was during 1958 that, after deliberation, I decided to try for further promotion. I had now reached the age of fifty and knew that my chances of getting a higher-ranking post would soon start to diminish, both on account of my age and the fact that the number of posts available was falling all the time. In view of the happy and interesting experiences I had had on the Relief Staff, my applications were confined to Relief Stationmaster posts. Another point that influenced my decision to some extent was that, apart from living in rented Station Houses, we had no settled home, as these houses almost invariably went with the post. It was time to make a fresh move.

CHAPTER 10

Relief Stationmaster — The Concluding Years

My first interview for a permanent post on the Relief Staff was at the District Operating Manager's office, at Wakefield. It was for a Relief Stationmaster's position in the Wakefield area, but on that occasion I was not the successful applicant. Shortly after this interview, I was summoned to attend another, again for a Relief Stationmaster's post, this time in the Hull area. The interviews were being taken by Mr C. Hearnshaw, who had recently been appointed District Operating Superintendent, after being Assistant Operating Manager in the Rotherham District. In fact, I had previously met Mr Hearnshaw at Sandal & Walton, before the station was absorbed into the Leeds district. The interview went very well and I was not really surprised to hear after a few days that I had been appointed to the post. This position on the Relief Staff was the summit of my ambition, and I was indeed grateful for having been selected.

My days at Walton were now numbered but, before I left, a surprise was in store for me. Mrs Iveson, on behalf of all my staff at Walton, presented me with a very useful carrying bag, for use when on the relief. It was partitioned into spaces for the various books and essentials one had to carry. It was touching to think that I had been remembered in this fashion.

My transfer from Walton took place some days afterwards, in October 1958. I had had a brief and cheery talk with Mr Hearnshaw before being "let loose" in the District. The Salaried Staff Clerk was a Mr Bill Bradley, and he gave me instructions to relieve the Stationmaster at Hedon on the Wednesday, Thursday and Friday and Bridlington on the Saturday, Monday and Tuesday. On Monday afternoon I travelled down to Hedon station to have a look round, and on Tuesday to Cottingham, to assess the chances of obtaining somewhere to stay. After much difficulty, Mr Jim Harvey, the Stationmaster there, secured some splendid lodgings for me, only three minutes' walk from the station. They were at the house of a Mrs Leach, who made me very welcome. At that time Mr Leach was a fireman with Hull Fire Brigade, and from time to time related thrilling and hair-raising stories of his experiences fire-fighting. Mr and Mrs Leach had a small market garden, with greenhouses, adjacent to the station. There they grew tomatoes and flowers, some of which I was able to take to my wife at Walton, at weekends when I was not on duty.

Referring back to Mr Harvey, it is interesting to note that he was Stationmaster at Upton & North Elmsall, the next station to Kirk Smeaton, during the latter part of my reign there! On Wednesday I reported to Hedon and was soon in the thick of things. In late 1958 Hedon station was still fully operational, with both goods and passenger services. The Stationmaster had no other responsibilities, that is no supervision of other stations, and a male clerk looked after the routine matters. Sack transactions were the big item here, with thousands of British Railways' grain sacks handled, both physically and on paper. The goods yard was busy with coal wagons and the movement of farm implements, which involved much cranage. Supervision of shunting was also a regular feature of the daily round.

On Saturday I travelled to Bridlington which, apart from Hull Paragon itself, was the largest station in the district. The Stationmaster's work here was entirely different from the usual routine, for during winter months he was responsible for matters affecting the seven Drivers stationed at Bridlington Motive Power Depot; this covered such items as work rosters, delays in running and the like. Steam locomotives had already been eliminated at Bridlington and the shed was more or less derelict. However, it was to remain in use at weekends in the summer months for some years to come. In a few short years the shed, like so many others, had become a ghost building, gaunt and empty.

One tried to imagine the dark, early mornings in winter, with engines being prepared in the gaslit shed for first turns. In howling wind, blizzard, fog, or pouring rain, the work went on. Belching smoke, then the muffled, subdued hiss of steam, ever-rising pressure showing on the gauges and an occasional spurt of steam from the safety valve of the foremost engine, indicating full pressure. The arrival of the first turn driver and fireman, the exchange of greetings, the stowing away in the cab of their "snap" bags and bottles of cold tea. For the driver a quick check of the engine mechanism and safety equipment, aided by the light of a guttering flare lamp. For the fireman a levelling of the fire, attention to the water levels and a final wipe of the regulator, handrails and so on. The mounting steam pressure becoming more and more evident, and the characteristic smell of warm lubricating oil permeating the cab. A glance at the ground signal controlling the exit from the shed, a heave on the regulator, and with steam shooting from the blow-off cocks, the engine ponderously making its way over the points, coming to a stand and finally backing on to its train in the bay platform, with early morning passengers already seated and others joining the train.

By 1958 all local passenger services were worked by diesel units, apart from the 9.07 am stopping train to Hull, which was the return working of the engine of the morning parcels train from Hull. Even this was soon to end. In the early morning, Bridlington station was quite busy with commuters, while the parcels side also dealt with substantial traffic. After the departure of the 8.52 for Hull comparative quietness returned. During the summer, of course, the pattern was much changed, especially at the weekends. The typing and routine matters in the Stationmaster's Office were dealt with by Miss M. Wadsley, who was also responsible for operating the train announcing system.

After finishing the relief at Bridlington, I went to North Ferriby, which at that time was not paired with any other station. Thereafter followed a session at Brough, relieving Mr Brown, the regular Stationmaster. Though smaller in size than Bridlington, Brough handled far more passengers and ranked second in the area, after Hull Paragon. In conversation with Mr Brown one day, I learned that recent censuses had shown that over a million passengers a year used the station. The great bulk of these were commuters, employed at the Blackburn Aircraft Works, which are situated quite near to the station. Brough Station in the late fifties was an entirely different proposition from what it was ten years later, but I will say more about that later.

One of the hazards of being on the Relief Staff, when working at stations where no clerk was employed, was locating particular items of stationery. Hard to find were such forms as "Application for a Situation", (very elusive this!) "BR Bank Paying-in or Withdrawal" forms, and other seldom used printings. It was a time-consuming job looking through drawers and cupboards and sometimes it was quicker to 'phone the neighbouring station and ask them to send a particular form on the next train! Some stations were easier to run than others in this respect. A "Where is it?" book did exist at a few stations and was a great help in locating items, provided it had been kept up to date. Incidentally, the "Where is it?" book was usually hung on a nail, above the ticket dating press, or inside the cash drawer, so that one could not fail to find it. While checking the stationery stocks at one station I came across some metal tubes, about the size of a pen holder; these, I recall, were issued in the years of the depression, to enable stubs of pencils to be fitted in the end, like a cigarette holder, so that they might be used up.

The period 1959-1970 was very important in every way to British Railways. Many changes were made in administration and the designation of staff; the design of uniform clothing was revolutionised; while the staff itself was reduced by several hundred thousand. Hundreds of stations and depots were closed down. In the Hull District spectacular changes and cuts were made. The old Hull and Barnsley line was an early victim of the economies, the whole of the main line being completely eliminated and the outward coal for shipment, works and domestic use diverted to the former North Eastern route, via Staddlethorpe Junction. I was in charge at Willerby & Kirkella, shortly before the line was closed. The beautifully constructed station was a typical example of sound workmanship, with a subway, lined with splendid glazed bricks, connecting the platforms, and platform awnings, as had most of the former Hull and Barnsley stations.

There were extensive domestic coal sales at Little Weighton and, to a lesser extent, at Willerby. While the run down was in progress, a goods train ran to Little Weighton, calling at Willerby & Kirkella. Practically all signalling was dispensed with, the signal box at Little Weighton serving as a ground frame for traffic purposes and the train being remarshalled in the rather large goods yard there, for the return trip. Near Little Weighton the towering cuttings, almost sheer and cut through solid rock, were a stark reminder of the obstacles encountered when the line was constructed in the 1880s. Most of the permanent way was in excellent order, having been relaid only a short time before closure, along with extensive renovation of signals and equipment, leading one to believe that a great deal of money had been wasted. Finally, as the rails were taken up by contractors, they were conveyed to Hull by special trains, a sad end indeed to the hopes of the Hull and Barnsley Railway promoters.

At the original interview with Mr Hearnshaw, in Hull, it was provisionally agreed that I would be allowed to reside at Goole, but my wife found much difficulty in obtaining a suitable house to purchase and, although we did finally secure a house, I incurred the wrath of my successor at Walton and the displeasure of Mr Hearnshaw, as at the time there was a wider choice in Hull. When we finally settled in I found that Goole made quite a good centre for covering the District. On one occasion, my third I believe when at Bridlington, my stay was marred by a derailment, which occurred at the wheel chock at the end of the coal depot cells. A hopper wagon loaded with coke mounted the wheel chock, rebounded and one pair of wheels left the track with the wagon heavily tilted. This could have been much worse, but it set the Hull Dairycoates breakdown gang quite a problem.

Filey was, understandably, a nice place to relieve at, especially during the summer, as one was able to get down to the Promenade during the meal interval. Flamborough and Bempton were under the control of one Stationmaster during my earlier years. Flamborough station was over two miles distant from the village of that name and, apart from the summer months, when there were many passengers from a caravan site near the station, patronage was very poor. The main traffic was in crabs, dispatched during the season mostly to the Midlands. The merchants and their customers certainly got crabs of first-class quality. Eventually Mr Baron, the Stationmaster at Flamborough, took responsibility for all the stations from Gristhorpe to Flamborough, including Filey, and, from then on, the job was a different proposition to relieve, requiring some planning to cover the work effectively.

Thursday was a sticky day, with each point from Sewerby Crossing to Gristhorpe to call at, with the wages. This involved a complicated arrangement of travelling by cycle, bus and ultimately walking. I can remember one particular occasion, after having eaten my snack with the signalman in the box at Speeton, walking along the track to Flamborough, as was my usual practice. Very heavy drizzle was falling at the time, and in the distance what appeared to be a dense fog drifting in from the direction of the cliff tops. I was soon set to rights on that score; it was falling rain! It was torrential. My shoes, trouser bottoms and hat were soaked through and through. There was no shelter, so on I trudged, the remarkable thing about it being that the rain ceased very quickly afterwards, and by the time I got to Flamborough I was almost dry. I was happy that there were no apparent ill effects.

The summit of the line, some 600 feet above sea level, is between Speeton and Bempton, which are almost three miles apart. This point is easily recognised by the presence of a permanent way hut. The site is a well-known danger spot during snow storms, the snow, having been blown in from the sea with terrific force, accumulating in the deep cuttings. To help prevent this happening, the fence rails have spaces on the seaward side. At Bempton there were quite a lot of blackberry bushes near to the track, with beautiful fruit! On the short distance of just over a mile between Flamborough station and Bempton the scenery changes rapidly although the gradient is rising all the way.

The Hull District covered quite a large area and among the most difficult parts to reach was that traversed by the Axholme Joint line. In the case of Reedness Junction it was necessary to make one's way from Goole by road, a distance of some six miles. I used my cycle on these journeys, and in winter it was quite a tough poroposition. Although the road was generally flat, the country was open to the full blast of everything the weather could offer. The final two miles were the worst and loneliest stretch. Short of Swinefleet village one turned very sharply right and, after roughly a further mile, it was then possible, on a clear day, to see the high water-tower at Reedness Junction from which the water cranes were supplied. The electric tablet and Tyer's Patent block instruments were at Reedness station office, the headquarters of the line. The main line split sharply, some 40 yds or so before reaching the lever box. The track to the left led to Fockerby terminus, which was in close proximity to the river Trent. Running over this 6½ miles long branch was governed by train staff (one engine in steam). The other branch of the fork ran to Epworth (Lincs), where the line terminated, the connection to Haxey Junction (Great Northern & Great Eastern Joint) having been severed some time previously. The electric tablet sections were from Marshland (on the Doncaster to Goole main line) to Reedness, Reedness to Crowle, Crowle to Belton and Belton to Epworth. There was no signalman at Reedness, or Epworth, and the Stationmasters, or Station Clerks, who had been passed in the Rules and Regulations, were responsible for working the block instruments, points and signals. The goods shunter stationed at Reedness travelled on the goods train to both Epworth and Fockerby, to assist the guard. In 1960 there were three Stationmasters on the branches, one each at Reedness Junction, Crowle and Epworth. Very soon the Crowle man was withdrawn, and some time later the Epworth Stationmaster, Mr Johnson, and his wife, who was Clerk at the station, suffered the same fate. This left the Stationmaster at Reedness, Mr G. Little, in full charge, with his wife as part-time clerk. The station house at Reedness was very isolated, with no piped water supply, or electric light. This was Kirk Smeaton all over again.

During the summer months traffic was fairly light, but from October to about late Spring there was quite a large quantity of agricultural traffic, both forwarded and received, in addition to domestic and coal inward and peat outward traffic. From end to end the Axholme Joint line boasted a large number of private sidings, and in the sugar beet season it was quite a job arranging wagons for loading and picking up, bearing in mind that some points to the main line faced one way and others the reverse. In this matter one had to rely on the travelling shunter and, of course, on 'phone messages from the traders.

It was at Reedness Junction where there occurred "The Unusual Case of the Locomotive that was Pushed to Start". The time was late afternoon towards the end of October. Much shunting had been done and most of the siding space was occupied by loaded wagons of sugar beet awaiting dispatch, many requiring labelling and checking. The heavily-laden train from Epworth was not long arrived when, after the first shunt, the driver of the six-coupled diesel locomotive announced with dismay that the engine had stalled. He was unable to restart and he wanted the diesel fitters to be sent from Goole Motive Power Depot. This was indeed a nasty one, it was almost five o'clock and I knew that the fitters at Goole would be on their way home. To send for them would mean long delay, as, in addition to collecting the men from their homes, transport to Reedness would have to be arranged. Seeing a fair number of agricultural workers engaged in loading sugar beet at the loading dock, an idea came into my head. I asked the driver whether he thought the engine would start if the locomotive were moved in gear. He said it might, but who would be likely to move it? I said that I would see what could be done and went across to the dock to ask the farm men if they would help me, after briefly explaining the position to them. There was ready agreement and, propelled by the united strenuous efforts of fourteen determined men, the recalcitrant monster started to move. With masterly judgement of the moment when 14 m.p. (i.e. manpower!) had reached maximum velocity, the driver let in the clutch and the engine burst into life with a mighty roar. It was a pleasing demonstration of what could be done, given the will, and, after thanking the men for their efforts, one of them laconically remarked that this was the first time that he had helped to push a railway engine! It was quite a new experience for me too!

Except for Hull Paragon, I worked at, or supervised, every station or depot in the Hull District. A fair amount of my time was spent at Market Weighton, which was a busy centre in the early sixties, many passengers having to change trains there. The York-Selby-Hull pick-up goods terminated at Market Weighton, and at times the scene in the goods yard was hectic. In both Selby and York directions the routes were fairly level throughout, but the lines to Hull and Driffield were quite sharply graded, particularly Enthorpe bank, on the latter. In fact, on Saturdays during the Summer season, an engine was despatched from Hull to stand pilot in the yard, until the last additional, or excursion, train had cleared the section. The station at Market Weighton was old and, with its classical portico facing the town, looked quite impressive. The huge Station House was attached to the main building, and was occupied by Mr Ron Jones, until the station and all the connecting lines were eliminated. Relief staff were always sure of a welcome jug of tea and often home-made cakes from Mrs Jones.

A rather unusual incident occurred on the Parcels side during one of my sessions at Market Weighton. Passenger parcels traffic for stations on the Derwent Valley Light Railway, which ran from the North Eastern station at Cliffe Common, near Selby, to York Layerthorpe, were held at

Market Weighton station daily, until the departure of the Selby pick-up goods. By a long-standing arrangement, the traffic was loaded into the tranship wagon, or guard's van, of the train, on arrival at the platform. On this particular morning there was quite a large quantity of parcels, ranging from mattresses, boxes of cake and tins of paint to day-old chicks. Owing to the cold weather the consignment of chicks had been placed in the porters room, for warmth and shelter. At noon I heard the pick-up goods stop and restart after the parcels had been loaded. Two minutes after this, Ivan, the porter, entered my room in a state of dismay. He had over-looked the unfortunate boxes of chicks and they had thus been left behind.

Well, here was a pretty kettle of fish, but with some presence of mind I rang up the Porter Signalman at Everingham, the first station on the Selby line, and told him to hold the goods there. This done, I went into the Station Cafe and Taxi Service premises. After explaining matters briefly I tentatively asked the Proprietor if he would be kind enough to take the chicks out to Everingham station in his taxi! The answer to this was that he most certainly would if possible, but his cafe was full of lunchtime customers. I offered to assist in his absence and my offer was accepted. He threw off his apron, the chicks were loaded on board and off he went to Everingham. I did what I could in the cafe and within thirty minutes he had returned and I think that, secretly, he had enjoyed his mission. He was pleased to inform me that the goods train was waiting and the chicks were now on their way. When I thanked him for his help in the matter, he refused to accept a penny piece for his services. This was very much a case of "all's well that ends well".

I spent some weeks at both Everingham, relieving Mr Benson, and Bubwith, in place of Mr Haigh; the latter was eventually moved to Driffield as Stationmaster. Before closure of the two stations, responsibility for both was transferred to Everingham. Stopping passenger trains had been withdrawn from the line in the fifties and the stations which remained open for goods traffic were not easy of access, although there was a bus service of sorts between Bubwith and Selby. By the time I went there, the bus services, which had been provided to replace the trains, had already been abandoned, through the lack of patronage in that sparsely-populated area. Between Bubwith and Market Weighton, the only other service available was the bus from Holme Moor to York, which covered some of the villages formerly touched upon by the Derwent Valley line, before its own passenger services were withdrawn in 1926. Incidentally, I can remember when the Derwent Valley Light Railway passenger service timetable, printed in bold red, white and blue letters, was posted up at some of the North Eastern Railway stations, at about the time of the Grouping.

Harvest time, especially in dry years, was always rather an anxious time to be relieving. There were still quite a few steam-hauled trains from Leeds and beyond to Bridlington and Scarborough, and sometimes a trail of fires followed each train, caused by sparks from the engine chimneys igniting the rank lineside growth. The old timber-built waiting room on the Selby platform at Everingham was gutted on one of these occasions. At the time there was quite a quantity of railway grain sacks stored inside. At Cliffe Common station a clerk was employed to calculate the toll charges and other work in connection with the passing of traffic to and from the Derwent Valley Light Railway, which was a privately-owned concern. Holme Moor also boasted a clerk, Mrs Rainforth, who was later transferred to Market Weighton. There was not much this lady did not know about clerical work at a country station!

Before I conclude my account of this portion of the District, I must relate what I shall term "The Mushroom Story". One morning in late August I had some cash to collect from Menthorpe Gate station. I therefore informed George Nicholson, Porter Signalman at Bubwith, what I was doing on the following morning, namely, walking from Menthorpe to Bubwith along the track. He told me the whereabouts of a field where mushrooms grew. I followed his instructions to the letter and picked about half a pound of splendid specimens, all that I could see round about. Later in the day, when I saw George, I showed them to him. He said that there ought to have been more than that and proved it the next day by picking a large carrier bag full. Magnificent! He said that I had not penetrated far enough into the field, and he was right. A few days later I was walking along the track, to one of the level crossings, when it came on to rain quite heavily. I dived into a field for shelter under some bushes for a few minutes and caught sight of what appeared to be a large, round, flat stone a few feet away. On closer investigation I found that it was a mushroom, nearly eight inches across. It was a perfect specimen, free from grubs, and my wife was delighted with it.

While at Cliffe Common one day, I witnessed the arrival of the goods train from York Layerthorpe Depot, on the Derwent Valley Light Railway, with quite a substantial train of loaded wagons. The locomotive was a J21 Class, 0-6-0, loaned from British Railways, as was the practice. It was in magnificent external condition, the paint and brasswork shining to absolute perfection. It must have been a joy for the Derwent Valley enginemen to handle and maintain such a grand machine!

It was indeed very sad to see the once busy station goods yards overgrown with weeds and the general air of dereliction that comes before a closure; also the once clean, light and cheerful station offices damp, dusty and mainly stripped of their moveable contents, a forlorn portent of the end of the railway for these places. The four intermediated stations were doomed, along with Market Weighton and Driffield themselves, and goods traffic was at a very low ebb. At the time of my retirement there were very few stations in the Hull District where goods traffic, in the proper sense of the term, was being handled at all. What few of the smaller stations are still open for passenger traffic have long since had their goods sidings removed, and the yards closed, to become merely unstaffed halts.

From time to time I covered the duties of the Stationmaster, and later Assistant Area Manager, at Goole. On one occasion this happened for a period of almost three months at a stretch, during the unfortunate illness of Mr Ted Ellis. With living in Goole it was, of course, very convenient, and I was able to cover any special arrangements without much difficulty. One of the outstanding railway engineering features of the Goole area is the huge swing bridge, spanning the Ouse, between Goole and Saltmarshe, on the Hull to Doncaster line. The bridge itself consists of a series of bow-string girder sections, the longest of which is the swinging portion. Perched on the top of it is the signal box controlling both rail movements and the actual opening of the bridge. When the bridge is swung, to allow the passage of river traffic, the signal box is cut off from the land by the swirling river. I have been inside the signal box several times when the bridge has been opened and the movment is very smooth throughout, the preliminary raising of the span by hydraulic power, to enable the huge locking bolts, at rail level, to be withdrawn, being the only signal that action is impending. The view after swinging is complete is indeed spectacular, with the rails ending in mid-air and the vessel passing far below. Included in the box's equipment is a megaphone and, what must be quite unique, a powerful telescope. Access to the box is gained by walking along the side of the track, to the centre of the swinging portion, then mounting the girder by an iron ladder. In foggy weather one has to exercise more than the usual care, since generally traffic travels over the bridge at speed, colour lights being installed. Substantial safety devices exist on each approach line to the bridge, with points to divert run-aways into sand drags — metal troughs filled with gravel over the rail tops. The movements of ships approaching the bridge are sometimes difficult to control, and careful judgement in the operation of the swinging portion is necessary.

It was during one of my periods at Goole that I was called upon to investigate a rather unusual derailment that had occurred early one morning. The vehicle involved was a bolster wagon, used for carrying girders, rails or long baulks of timber. It had travelled from Hull, apparently without incident, until a chain, which was part of the wagon equipment, had fallen through a hole in the floor of the wagon and trailed over the rail. One of the wagon's wheels had run over it, being derailed in the process. Shortly after this, trailing points which of course were closed, leading from the goods yard to the main line, formed a "Vee" into which the derailed wheels ran. This forced the wheels upwards and, although the switch blade was strained, the wheels re-mounted the rails. This was the first experience I had had of such a happening, though I had heard of similar incidents. The dragging chain later became caught in the points at Boothferry Road Crossing and broke. Apart from a few scarred sleepers and the strained points, there was no apparent damage.

Invariably, when adjoining stations were placed under the supervision of one Stationmaster, the accounts of the subsidiary station were merged with those of the parent station, which became responsible for the production of the monthly figures. Over the years the method of dealing with passenger parcels traffic gradually changed. In my early days at Kirk Smeaton, parcels accepted from the public were charged according to the weight and distance cards provided. They were then franked with pasted-on charges stamps, printed in denominations ranging from 1d to

£1, accounting books being provided to record the daily balance. Firstly, to save printing costs, the charges stamps were withdrawn and blanks, for completion in ink, substituted. Finally, even these were dispensed with, and replaced by entry sheets, on which all items were recorded, cash being taken in the normal way, but all the sheets, whether cash or credit, were sent at that time to the Accounting Centre at Doncaster. Constant changes were also being introduced in all branches of passenger ticket accountancy, together with succeeding sets of forms to accommodate the amended procedures. Other than a growing demoralisation and cynicism amongst station clerical staff, it was extremeley difficult to see what was accomplished by all these changes; but at least they helped to prevent redundancy in the Railway's Printing Department. From my earliest days visits from the District Auditor, or his Assistant, were a regular feature at all stations, but in the middle sixties these visits were curtailed, no doubt to cut costs. Instead, one could expect spot checks to be made at any time.

Staff paybill work, in itself quite involved, was originally performed manually throughout, full-time pay-clerks being employed at all the larger stations. Pay-as-you-earn and National Insurance deductions were dealt with at the same time; pay slips also had to be prepared locally. All this was cut out in the late sixties, after a computer had been installed at Darlington Paybill Office. Time sheets, submitted by all stations and depots, were fed into the machine, which then printed out the payroll, together with tear-off pay slips, showing all deductions, etc. These were sent to the individual stations in time for pay day. Making up the actual pay packets remained, of course, the responsibility of the station concerned.

From 1962, when the Beeching era began, every activity was critically examined, and ever-more stringent economies introduced: almost total closure of the former Hull and Barnsley main line; abandonment of yards and tracks in the Hull Docks area; "Pay Trains" taking over on the Hull-Hornsea and Hull-Withernsea branches, with the consequent withdrawal of all ticket issuing facilities at the intermediate stations, and redundancy for their staffs. Even these economies, however, did not prevent total closure of both lines only a few years later, but it is more than possible that the operating expenses of the level crossings at Botanic Gardens, Stepney, Southcoates and other points, may have been the decisive factor.

Having watched the dramatic changes in staff clothing since nationalisation, readers may perhaps wonder what were the opinions of the people who had to wear it. My own remarks must be confined very largely to the uniform provided for Stationmaster, and later Area Manager and Assistant Area Manager grades. My first uniform, issued to me at Kirk Smeaton in 1943, had a single-breasted jacket, of close-texture, navy blue serge and a hard-top cap of the same material, with the words "Station Master", woven in gold silk, on the band. There is no doubt in my mind that this issue was the smartest and most comfortable uniform that I ever wore, and for many years after that, indeed up to the late sixties, both quality and style steadily deteriorated. Double-breasted jackets were issued at a time when the fashion was on its way out. The original neat cap was changed for a heavier type of headgear, with lavish gold wire and ornate badge, which was a menace in windy weather. I remember the late Walter Baron, Stationmaster at Filey, telling me that he was once at Hunmanby station, supervising the seating of the girls from Hunmanby High School, when a particularly strong gust of wind blew off his uniform hat like a rising kite. Finally it rolled along the platform edge on to the line, to the accompaniment of loud laughter from the waiting females. One can imagine the chagrin of the wearer!

In the late sixties the blue uniforms were abandoned in favour of the present grey continental style. From the outset I considered these outfits to be poor and wearing them only confirmed my suspicions. The old-fashioned double-breasted style was perpetuated, the cloth seeming to gather every speck of grime. It was impossible to retain any crease in the trousers. The pill-box type hat, with soft top and sides, though comfortable to wear, was not much use in wet weather for, when soaked, the water funnelled down the back of one's neck. At least the old mortar boards had the merit of throwing off the wet on to one's mackintosh.

There was one Stationmaster's position in the District which was quite unique. This was the post at Hull (Corporation Pier), some twenty minutes' walk from Hull Paragon. One point was that it was a station without trains, though some of the responsibilities of the Stationmaster were naturally the same as at an ordinary railway station. The Booking Office held quite a large stock of tickets, including rail tickets to stations in Lincolnshire and beyond. The charge for conveyance across the Humber of private motor cars and smaller commercial vehicles was assessed on the length of the wheelbase, the tickets being of a brick red or pink colour. These were of Edmonson type, dated and issued in the same way as ordinary railway tickets. There were often latecomers, especially for the morning sailings, and sometimes it was not possible to ship the car on the next crossing, owing to the lack of room on deck. Passenger accommodation was always adequate for requirements, either on deck, or in the saloon. If cars were left behind on one particular sailing, the Stationmaster had to assess the situation quickly, in order to decide whether an extra trip was justified for the traffic offering. The critical figure was normally no less than six cars. If an extra journey was laid on, the Captains on the two ferries maintaining the service had to be informed promptly. Word was passed to the Captain of the next arriving ferry to work an extra trip immediately the cars were loaded, while New Holland was told by telephone to get the other ferry back as quickly as possible, to work the scheduled service from Hull. Afterwards, further adjustments were made to the trips, to restore the scheduled workings.

Much has been written about the "Castles", the three paddle steamers which maintain the service between Hull and New Holland. Sufficient for me to say that, in my opinion, the boats represented all that was best in steam-driven vessels, the service generally was reliable and the boats were spotlessly clean. If the service was delayed, it was usually due to exceptionally low tides, which could extend the normal twenty minutes journey time. Saturday was the busiest day for passengers, in both directions, and probably Monday for motor vehicles. When on duty the Parcels Foreman gave the signal for the boats to leave the stage; the Travelling Ticket Collector, at the barrier to the pontoon, then walked along to the boat and, after he had joined the vessels, the gangway was raised and the boat cast off. The leading porters were responsible for casting off the boats on departure and for mooring them on arrival and, believe me, these jobs could be tricky when there was a heavy swell, or a rough sea. All the posts, outdoors at any rate, had a nautical flavour. The station building was quite impressive in its way, the Stationmaster's house being incorporated in the block. The premises were very lofty, with some Great Central characteristics. The pair of folding steps, kept in the station entrance lobby, were the largest and probably the heaviest in Europe! The Stationmaster's office was situated on the first floor and had a nice view over the Humber. My periods of deputising for Mr Allott, the Stationmaster, were not without incident, as the following story will show.

As already mentioned, the usual signal to the ferry crew to start the sailing was when the travelling ticket collector joined the ship. On this particular morning there was an extra travelling collector from Lincoln on duty at the barrier, for the purpose of a special ticket check. For some reason or other, he left the barrier a few minutes before sailing time and joined the ferry. On seeing the Ticket Collector approaching, and obviously not consulting their watches, the staff raised the gangway and the boat was cast off. A long and powerful blast from the steam hooter and the boat was under way. This was indeed a surprise. I was in Nelson Street at the time and, along with the other "ground staff", was certainly taken aback. The Corporation bus from the City had just arrived, with quite a large number of passengers, including a contingent of girls from Hunmanby Hall School for Lincoln and other places. Something had to be done quickly. The Resident Ticket Collector and I tore down the gangway to the stage, and with whistles blowing and newspapers waving we caught the Captain's attention. The river boiled and eddied as the paddles were put into reverse, and the vessel returned to the pier, to allow the now anxious passengers to board her. Many would have been stranded for some hours at the other side had the connection not been made. Not all the trips, however, had distant rail connections. In addition to car and passenger traffic, mid-week saw vast quantities of meat, fish and greengroceries from Hull wholesale market, being shipped across the Humber; these goods were brought down to the station on four-wheeled barrows. Fog and sea mist could be a great menace and I have more than once heard a Captain say that fitting Radar to the boats was the most welcome change that ever happened to them.

Next to Brough, the stations with the largest numbers of commuters were Beverley, Cottingham, Ferriby, Hessle and, of course, Goole. Upwards of three hundred passengers travelled from Cottingham into Hull before 9.00 am every weekday. I spent quite some time at Cottingham

78

and was always pleased to be sent there. The station was kept very clean and the gardens here, and at Beverley, were always likely prize-winners. During the period the late Harold Burton was Leading Porter at the station, the General Waiting Room fire on the Down platform must have been the largest on British Railways! It was lit at 6.00 am and piled so high with coal, that it scarcely needed attention before the change of shifts at 2.00 pm.

In the course of my duties on the Hull and Barnsley section, I remember once relieving Mr Norman Avery who was at North Cave, but was also in charge of Sandholme & Wallingfen. It was pay-day and, following established practice, the Engineers Department Ganger took me to Sandholme on his petrol-driven motor trolley, which was mainly used for conveying men to lineside work sites. These trolleys were called "pneumonia" wagons (pronounced pee-new-monia) by some of the Engineer's staff, on account of the exposed and draughty ride they gave! The journey to Sandholme went without incident, but about a mile after leaving on the return the engine died on us and nothing would induce it to re-start. The result was that we had to push it back to Sandholme, a distance of nearly four miles and a very frustrating end to the outing.

The last three days of my active service were spent at Goole, relieving Mr Ellis, and 23rd September 1970 was The Day. After that, I took some lieu days, that is, days owing to me, for working on public holidays. The Hull District Office was now virtually closed and for the last three weeks of my service I was under the Divisional Manager, Doncaster. My wife and I said goodbye to Mr Lewis, Assistant to Mr Reid, the Divisional Manager, in his office, on Friday 9th October. Thus, after 47 years, my railway career ended, hastened by my being made redundant, as ever fewer posts were left to be filled.

Generally, the Beeching era, from 1962 onwards, was not a happy one, for while Merry-go-round and Liner trains, and special vehicles to convey motor cars and other commodities in bulk, proved to be profitable ventures, the uncertainty of continued employment ravaged Staff morale. Many excellent men left the Service, to take up outside employment, creating vacancies which could not be filled. No-one will ever know how much this cost British Railways, but the wage bill alone was inflated astronomically as vacant posts had to be covered by vastly expensive overtime working, often for periods of many months until decisions were reached and the future of stations and depots decided. The running down of many country lines, most of which had never been really profitable, even before the motor car, together with services which were not convenient to the travelling public, and which in some cases were not suitable to the needs of secondary school children attending school, all made closures inevitable.

All three stations where I served as Stationmaster — Kirk Smeaton, Rye Hill & Burstwick and Sandal & Walton — have been completely closed, as have quite a large number of those where I relieved.

All in all, a rather sad postscript to the story of a working life which brought much contentment and satisfaction and left one feeling at the end that one had been a member of a good team, doing a worthwhile job and had seen it well done.